Rising Roles in Law

Designing the AI-Enabled, Data-Driven Law Firm

EDITED BY FRANCESCA RAMADAN

Commissioning editor
Francesca Ramadan

Managing director
Sian O'Neill

Rising Roles in Law: Designing the AI-Enabled, Data-Driven Law Firm
is published by

Globe Law and Business Ltd
3 Mylor Close
Horsell
Woking
Surrey GU21 4DD
United Kingdom
Tel: +44 20 3745 4770
www.globelawandbusiness.com

Rising Roles in Law: Designing the AI-Enabled, Data-Driven Law Firm

ISBN 978-1-83723-200-0
EPUB ISBN 978-1-83723-201-7
Adobe PDF ISBN 978-1-83723-202-4

GPSR Compliance: EU Authorised Representative: Easy Access System Europe – Mustamäe tee 50, 10621 Tallinn, Estonia, gpsr.requests@easproject.com

Contents

Executive summary

Artificial intelligence (AI) is transforming the legal profession at an unprecedented pace, but it is not technology alone that is reshaping law firms. Equally significant is the emergence of an entirely new class of professionals responsible for designing, implementing, governing, and scaling AI-enabled legal services. As clients demand greater efficiency, transparency, and commercial value, and as alternative legal service providers, AI-native firms, and multidisciplinary competitors continue to expand, traditional partnership models are being fundamentally reimagined. Today's leading firms are no longer built solely around lawyers; they increasingly depend upon legal engineers, data scientists, knowledge professionals, legal operations specialists, AI governance experts, product managers, and other interdisciplinary professionals whose expertise extends well beyond conventional legal practice.

Despite the rapid emergence of these roles, many firms remain uncertain about how they should be structured, integrated, and developed. Organizations are investing heavily in AI technologies, but often lack the structural frameworks, governance models, and talent strategies needed to translate technological capability into sustainable competitive advantage. While numerous books explore artificial intelligence or legal technology, few examine the people responsible for delivering these transformations or the operating models required to support them. *Rising Roles in Law: Designing the AI-Enabled, Data-Driven Law Firm* fills that gap, bringing together leading in-house and law firm practitioners, legal technologists, and consultants to examine the emerging professions shaping the future of legal services.

We begin by stepping back to examine the broader forces driving this transformation. In Chapter 1, Ken Crutchfield, founder and CEO of Spring Forward Consulting, explores how AI has become a catalyst for structural change across the legal industry. He examines the growing influence of corporate legal departments, alternative legal service providers, private equity investment, and AI-native law firms, arguing that these developments are fundamentally redefining the boundaries of legal practice and creating the conditions for entirely new professional roles. By establishing the market, commercial, and technological context underpinning this transformation, this chapter demonstrates why multidisciplinary expertise will become central to the future of the modern law firm.

Having established why law firms must evolve, Chapter 2, authored by Ali Chaudhry, senior legal engineer at Simmons & Simmons, turns to one of the profession's most significant emerging roles: the legal engineer. Drawing on his own experience as a practicing legal engineer, Ali traces the evolution of the discipline from Richard Susskind's early conception of the legal knowledge engineer to the sophisticated legal engineering functions operating within today's leading firms. The chapter explains what legal engineers actually do in practice – from process mapping, requirements gathering, and change management to productizing legal services and bridging the gap between lawyers and technologists – and examines how firms can structure these functions to maximize value. It provides both practitioners and law firm leaders with a practical understanding of one of the fastest-growing professions in legal services.

Continuing our exploration of the emerging AI-enabled workforce, Chapter 3, authored by Matthew J. Dunne, AI solutions lead at K&L Gates LLP, examines the rise of legal data scientists and analytics professionals. While legal engineers focus on designing systems and workflows, data scientists generate the insights that enable firms to make better operational and strategic decisions. Matthew explores how data science is transforming legal practice through dashboards, automation, natural language processing, and advanced analytics, while acknowledging the inherent limitations of predictive modelling in complex legal environments. The chapter argues that data science should not replace professional judgment, but instead strengthen it by introducing greater consistency, transparency, and evidence-based decision-making, ultimately laying the foundations for what the author terms "legal intelligence".

Knowledge lies at the heart of every successful AI initiative. In Chapter 4, Colin S. Levy, general counsel at Malbek, explores the increasingly strategic role of knowledge management in AI-enabled legal practice, demonstrating why effective AI depends not only on sophisticated technology, but also on well-governed, structured, and accessible knowledge. The chapter examines the rise of prompt engineering, the governance of institutional knowledge, and the growing importance of feedback systems that enable AI capabilities to improve over time. Drawing upon examples of both successful implementations and highly publicized failures, Colin argues that sustainable AI adoption is fundamentally a knowledge management challenge. He concludes by examining the emergence of client-facing AI applications and the governance responsibilities that accompany them.

Our attention then turns to legal operations, one of the fastest-growing service areas within modern legal practice. In Chapter 5, Katie Moon, head of legal design and operations, and Daniel Solomon, portfolio lead: client collaboration at Lewis Silkin LLP, examine how legal operations has evolved from a niche support function into a strategic discipline that enables both law firms and their clients to deliver legal services more efficiently. Framed through the interconnected themes of people, process, data, and technology, the chapter explores the skills required of legal operations professionals; the work they perform; and the growing influence of AI on operational delivery. Katie and Daniel also consider how forward-thinking firms are productizing legal operations as a client-facing service, enabling them to move beyond traditional legal advice and deliver broader operational value.

As AI becomes embedded throughout legal practice, governance has become just as important as innovation. In Chapter 6, Harry Borovick, general counsel at Luminance, and Amy Merrick, senior legal counsel at Google DeepMind, examine the emergence of the AI governance professional and argue that many AI failures stem not from technology itself, but from inadequate governance. Drawing on recent legal developments and practical experience, the chapter introduces a robust "four gate" governance framework covering tool selection, matter suitability, output verification, and organizational change management. Alongside discussions of legal professional privilege, cybersecurity, client expectations, and commercial pressures, Harry and Amy demonstrate that effective governance provides the essential infrastructure that enables firms to adopt AI responsibly, confidently, and at scale.

The successful implementation of AI requires more than individual specialists – it depends upon teams capable of combining diverse expertise. In Chapter 7, Dr Catriona Wolfenden, director of product and innovation at Weightmans LLP, explores how law firms can build high-performing multidisciplinary teams that integrate lawyers, technologists, product specialists, knowledge professionals, and operational experts. Drawing on her experience leading the evolution of Weightmans' Product and Innovation function, she examines the skills, organizational structures, leadership models, and cultural factors that underpin successful collaboration. Particular attention is given to the shift from isolated innovation projects towards product-led legal services and the organizational changes required to support this transition. The chapter concludes with practical lessons on building teams that are capable not only of developing innovative solutions, but also of delivering lasting organizational change.

Looking beyond individual roles, Chapter 8, authored by Olga V. Mack, CEO of TermScout, argues that the legal profession is undergoing a more fundamental transformation than the emergence of new job titles alone might suggest. Rather, law firms are moving from document-centric legal practice towards system-driven legal decision-making. Through a series of practical frameworks – including the concept of the Legal Decision Stack and the Risk-Tiered Action Model – Olga demonstrates how legal engineers, knowledge professionals, data specialists, and AI governance leaders each contribute to the design, implementation, and monitoring of legal decision systems. By reframing contracts, litigation artefacts, and legal workflows as components of ongoing decision infrastructure, rather than static documents, this chapter offers readers a compelling vision of how AI-enabled legal organizations will increasingly operate.

We conclude by returning to the human capabilities that underpin every successful transformation. In Chapter 9, managing knowledge lawyer at Lewis Silkin LLP, Paul Caddy examines the skills, behaviors, and organizational culture required to support the AI-enabled law firm. While technology has become increasingly sophisticated, its successful adoption ultimately depends upon people. Paul identifies the technical, commercial, and behavioral capabilities that professionals across law firms must develop – including AI literacy, prompt engineering, critical thinking, legal risk awareness, curiosity, and adaptability – and explores how firms can create cultures that encourage experimentation while maintaining appropriate governance. Emphasizing that AI adoption is fundamentally a change management challenge, rather than a technology challenge, he concludes by arguing that capability development must become an ongoing organizational priority if firms are to realize AI's full potential.

Together, these chapters demonstrate that the future of legal practice will be shaped not simply by the technologies firms adopt, but by the people, structures, and multidisciplinary capabilities they build around them. *Rising Roles in Law: Designing the AI-Enabled, Data-Driven Law Firm* offers a practical roadmap for understanding this changing professional landscape, equipping law firm leaders, innovation professionals, and legal practitioners with the insight needed to design, develop, and lead the AI-enabled, data-driven law firm of the future.

About the contributors

Harry Borovick is the general counsel and AI governance officer at Luminance, where he leads the global legal and company secretarial function of a fast-growing legal tech company. He is also a professor (hon.) and the program director of the AI Governance Leadership Programme (AIGLP) at King's College London, where he teaches AI governance, ethics, and practical AI risk management in legal practice.

He is a LexLab research fellow at UC Law San Francisco and a lecturer at Queen Mary University of London and at Barbri Global. He also sits as a member of the Technology Group of the Chartered Institute of Arbitrators (CIArb), co-authoring their guidelines on AI in arbitration. Most recently, Harry co-authored a chapter on AI in legal practice in the *IAPP AIGP Artificial Intelligence Governance Professional Study Guide* (2026).

Paul Caddy is a commercial, technology, and data protection lawyer whose career has spanned traditional legal practice, in-house roles, and the ever-evolving intersection of law and technology. He currently works at Lewis Silkin, where he specializes in technology and AI law. Previously, Paul was head of insight at a major UK law firm and worked in-house at a large global events business. In 2023, Paul co-authored *Legal Practice in the Digital Age* (2023), and is a recognized voice on technology, innovation, and the human aspects of technological change. He has spoken at numerous events, including the Westminster Legal Policy Forum and Future Lawyer. He is a member of the Law Society of England and Wales' AI Steering Group. He also serves on the TEDLaw International Advisory Board and the Advisory Panel at Damar Training. In 2025, he completed Imperial Business School's executive course on AI for Business Innovation.

Ali Chaudhry is a senior legal engineer at Simmons & Simmons, working within the firm's Applied AI team. He focuses on the design and deployment of AI tools for legal teams, working across AI adoption strategy, generative AI applications, and targeted upskilling for lawyers and clients. He has supported organizations across sectors with responsible AI adoption through solution design, training, and strategic implementation, and has delivered bespoke large language model solutions for both internal and client use.

His background is in legal academia, where his research focused on the intersection of law and AI. He holds a particular interest in advanced AI capabilities, including retrieval-augmented generation, prompt engineering and agentic systems, and their practical application in legal and regulatory contexts.

Ken Crutchfield is the founder and CEO of Spring Forward Consulting, an advisory business that serves legal technology businesses and consults on artificial intelligence.

He has over 40 years of experience in legal, tax, and other industries. Throughout his career, he has focused on growth, innovation, and business transformation. As a strategic thinker who understands markets and the creation of products to meet customer needs, he has worked in start-ups and large enterprises. He has served in general management capacities in six businesses.

Ken has a pulse on the trends affecting the market. Whether it was the Internet in the 1980s or generative AI, he understands technology and how it can impact business, industry, and the practice of law.

Crutchfield started his career with LexisNexis and has worked at Thomson Reuters, Bloomberg, Dun & Bradstreet, and Wolters Kluwer. Ken has an MBA and holds a Bachelor of Science in Electrical Engineering from The Ohio State University.

Matthew Dunne is the AI solutions lead at K&L Gates LLP. In his role, Matthew helps attorneys and allied professionals implement AI into their work, measure value and profitability, and win new business. Matthew holds a Master of Science in Applied Data Science from the University of Chicago and a Juris Doctor from Indiana University Maurer School of Law. He is also a licensed attorney.

Colin S. Levy is a lawyer, legal technology strategist, and author who has spent more than a decade working at the intersection of legal practice and innovation. He serves as general counsel and evangelist at Malbek, a contract lifecycle management platform, and teaches Technology and Law Practice Management as an adjunct professor at Albany Law School. He also sits on the Board of Directors of the Corporate Legal Operations Consortium (CLOC).

One of the most recognized voices in the legal tech world, Colin writes for Law360, Bloomberg Law, and Law.com, and speaks widely on how lawyers can engage with emerging technology thoughtfully and without fear. He is the author of *The Legal Tech Ecosystem*, co-author of *CLM for Dummies*, and editor of the *Handbook of Legal Tech*.

Colin holds a Bachelor of Arts from Trinity College and a Juris Doctor from Boston College Law School. He lives in Great Barrington, Massachusetts.

Olga V. Mack is a CEO, legal technologist, and former general counsel focused on the intersection of law, technology, and business operations. She currently serves as CEO of TermScout, a contract intelligence company that benchmarks and certifies contract terms using structured data and market signals. Olga is also the creator of ESI Flow, a workflow tool designed to bring structure and decision clarity to eDiscovery negotiations. A fellow at CodeX, The Stanford Center for Legal Informatics, Olga writes and speaks about how AI is reshaping legal systems, governance, and decision-making across organizations.

Amy Merrick is a senior lawyer at Google DeepMind, operating at the forefront of global AI governance and regulation. She specializes in navigating the complex intersections of frontier technology, public policy, and risk management, advising on strategic consultations with international governments and translating evolving hard and soft law into practical operational frameworks. Bridging practice and academia, Amy also lectures on AI governance at King's College London.

Katie Moon is a commercial lawyer who specializes in alternative legal services, including legal design and legal operations. She is currently head of legal design and operations at Lewis Silkin, where she leads the team delivering innovative projects to in-house legal clients. Her expertise in this area grew in her role as a senior legal counsel at TLB, an alternative legal services provider, where she was one of the creators of oneNDA, a standardized, automation-friendly, and largely non-negotiable NDA that has been adopted by thousands of companies worldwide. She has spoken at Legal Geek about the benefits of simplified contracts and legal processes, and is passionate about cutting through the complexities of dense legal jargon to create accessible and user-friendly contracts and policies. She is also an advocate for leveraging technology in manual legal processes and continues to support her clients throughout their legal transformation initiatives.

Daniel Solomon has worked in the legal field for ten years. Having initially followed the traditional route of paralegalling, with the aim of becoming a lawyer, Daniel pivoted towards legal operations and technology in 2018, with an initial focus on contract lifecycle management, and hasn't looked back since. He has worked at Lewis Silkin since 2020 and has helped support the firm in its transition to becoming a technology-enabled law firm by playing a key role in selecting, implementing, and embedding the firm's AI, automation, and client extranet technology stack. He and his team have worked closely with co-author Katie Moon, providing support on the technology side of legal operations work. Daniel has represented the firm at industry events, webinars, and roundtables, and was formerly a member of the City of London Corporation's Lawtech Sounding Board.

Catriona Wolfenden is an equity partner and product and innovation director at Weightmans LLP, where she leads the delivery of product and innovation initiatives aligned to client needs and firm strategy. An accidental lawyer who fell into innovation, she has built an award-winning team and was recognized in The Lawyer Hot 100 in 2025. With a background in law and knowledge management, she is particularly interested in the skills future lawyers will need to cultivate in an increasingly AI-enabled workplace. Alongside her role at Weightmans, Catriona is a visiting professor at Edge Hill University Business School, working with the School of Law and Criminal Justice to support applied research and impact in AI, legal tech, and digital business. She is a former director of UK LegalTech Association and a current member of the UK Research and Innovation (UKRI) Future Leaders Fellowships (FLF) Panel College. She also sits on the UK AI Industry Association (UKAI) Legal Working Group, and co-authored *Innovation in Law Firms: Implementing Successful Projects* (2024), published by Globe Law and Business.

Chapter 1: The changing structure of the modern, AI-enabled law firm

By Ken Crutchfield, founder and CEO, Spring Forward Consulting

ChatGPT took the world by storm when OpenAI released it in November 2022. Within two months, the generative artificial intelligence (AI) service had garnered 100 million registered users, marking the shortest timeframe to reach that milestone.[1] For comparison, it took 16 years for the iPhone to reach the same, and TikTok took nine months.

Not only could ChatGPT provide very comprehensive and convincing answers to questions, but it also truly mastered the nuances of language. It could explain Einstein's theory of relativity as a poem, translate from one language, or simplify an explanation of a complex topic.[2] The world took notice and, for the first time in memory, managing partners at the largest of the BigLaw firms paid attention to the impact of technology on their business. It's not that firms had ignored technology before, but this represented an existential threat. Could AI actually disrupt legal? In response, Goldman Sachs put out a report suggesting that 44 percent of all legal work could be automated by AI.[3]

Firms have been under pressure for years from clients to be more efficient, and the COVID-19 lockdowns accelerated digital trends already in play by pushing more work online. Laggards who held on to paper-based approaches for collaboration were forced to give them up, and Zoom meetings are now as normal as face-to-face interaction. ChatGPT added fuel to the fire, with promises of both productivity improvement and disruption. Chief innovation officers emerged in BigLaw, and the knowledge management (KM) and IT staff were inundated with trials and evaluations of the latest technology offerings.

Despite the efficiencies of accelerated technology adoption, the demand within the legal industry continues to grow. Latest figures from the US show 8 percent growth for 2024, with no slowdown.[4] Courts have increasing backlogs. The most recent statistics from California suggest that 4.8 million cases were filed in Superior Courts, with close to one million cases added to the backlog, net of depositions.[5]

Additionally, while hard to measure, latent demand also exists for legal services, as consumers and businesses alike forego the use of attorneys.[6] Small businesses face the decision of whether to seek legal assistance before signing a contract or making a strategic business decision, given the expense. Growing businesses operate across more jurisdictions and must decide when and how to comply with the ever-expanding scope of laws and regulations each year.

Corporate clients as catalysts for change

Businesses are the primary clients of large law firms. They pay the bills, and changes in how they spend ripple across the ecosystem. Many law departments have legal operations teams that help reevaluate processes to define "better, faster, and more efficient" ways to complete work. They are deploying ticketing systems and options to help internal customers serve themselves. For example, a business unit may create a non-disclosure agreement, have it e-signed, and route it to a central repository, where all documents are tagged by legal entity and counterparty for later retrieval.

They are also reconsidering what might be better accomplished in-house, given automation, rather than seeking outside counsel. New areas of compliance, such as the General Data Protection Regulation, start with a firm's expertise and, over time, become operationalized within the business. However, maintenance of corporate registrations, trademark renewals, and copyright filings might be better handled by a legal services provider that offers productized services, rather than by a law firm that has handled these tasks for decades. Corporations are reducing the number of firms they work with and want to rely on a smaller set of strategic firms that can serve them across many practice areas and disciplines.[7] They expect those firms to understand their businesses better and provide consistent, coordinated service. Rather than individual practice area silos, they want law firms to serve them across practice areas and matters as a single firm.

At the same time, corporations themselves must control costs, and they are very strict about what a firm can and cannot charge. These are called outside counsel guidelines (OCGs), and they frequently restrict firms from charging for items like legal research, the time of a first-year associate, or work that should reasonably be automated using AI. The implicit message is to encourage firms to operate with low overhead and greater efficiency in their client-facing engagements. It is up to the firm to determine how to invest in training staff and stay current technologically. Ironically, the inability to recover those items reinforces the billable-hour business model, which forces rates higher to cover non-billable overhead and investment.

The new competitive landscape

Work that moves in-house is more about optimizing who does the work best and is a natural part of the lifecycle for some legal tasks, such as compliance. When more repeatable or commoditized work moves in-house, it is likely welcomed by firms, given the low margins. With growth in the overall market and latent demand, there are opportunities to fill the void.

Client decisions that can negatively impact a law firm occur when the client directs work to a legal service provider or an AI-native law firm. Private equity and venture capital are fueling greater competition from these categories.

Legal service providers

Alternative legal service providers (ALSPs) offer services that may require legal know-how, but do not fall under the regulatory oversight of law firms for legal advice.[8] ALSPs are becoming mainstream, and perhaps they should not be deemed "alternative" anymore, given that they account for about five percent of worldwide legal spend.[9] The legal services category is growing faster than law firms, with the most recent studies suggesting annual growth rates approaching 20 percent.[10]

Legal service providers are organized as corporations and rely more on technology and low-cost staff to perform certain functions, such as reviewing contracts or documents in eDiscovery. For contract review, an understanding of the law is required, but workflows and rules can be defined to manage the work, with automation technology, low-cost staff, or AI agents. If a contract does not conform to defined rules or checklists, it can be flagged for review by a licensed attorney working on behalf of the service provider or the customer. The same can hold true for the extensive review of documents under eDiscovery.

The role of private equity

Private equity is looking to invest in legal services and the broader legal market. In the US, the American Bar Association's Model Rule 5.4 requires that law firms be owned only by lawyers for independence and ethical reasons.[11] Several jurisdictions in the US are experimenting with non-lawyer ownership structures, known as alternative business structures (ABS). In Arizona, there are over 150 ABS law firms now registered. In 2001, Australia was the first country to establish an ABS regime.[12] In 2007, the UK passed the Legal Services Act, which created the opportunity for non-lawyer ownership of law firms and legal services, too.[13] These programs provide a vehicle for investment and experimentation in non-lawyer ownership. That opens the door to more private equity and venture capital, and to greater competition with traditional law firms.

There are several ways that private equity is looking to invest in the legal industry. The first is through legal service providers via managed services organizations (MSOs) that provide productized legal services.[14] Renovus Capital recently formed an MSO with over $400 million in revenue.[15] When compared with US law firms, it would rank alongside BigLaw peers in the middle of the top 200. A second way is by helping firms tease out their non-legal functions, such as marketing, accounting, HR, and research. With creative structuring, these non-legal functions can accept investment and provide better services to the law firm.

The private equity model is most attractive to firms with a higher proportion of expenses not directly tied to legal advice. Collective action firms in the UK and their mass tort and class action counterparts in the US and Australia are the most likely to be the first to be attracted to private equity investment. Costly tasks such as client communication and collecting medical history updates do not require an attorney and are ripe for optimization.

Private equity will begin to standardize these non-legal functions and drive efficiencies and, with the ABS model opening up in the US, private equity and venture capital will both look to test the boundaries of non-lawyer ownership of law firms more aggressively.

The Uber moment: The unauthorized practice of law

AI chatbots are driving self-service as a substitute for seeking legal advice and providing greater access to justice. Consumers are using AI as a substitute for lawyers and even winning arguments in court.[16] Hallucinations remain a challenge for consumers in particular, but the wave of consumer use of AI draws parallels to Uber's growth. In the US, Uber captured the hearts of riders well before the rideshare service was on the regulatory horizon. By the time regulators understood what was happening, regulation was driven by politics and consumer value, rather than the protection of the legacy "taxi cartel".

Legal is having an Uber moment. There are legitimate questions about whether an AI chatbot can provide legal advice. Objectively, they do. The services provide value to consumers who could not otherwise afford a lawyer, and lawyers also use professional-grade legal AI tools that use the same underlying language models.

With AI chatbots capable of providing legal advice, and non-lawyer ownership of law firms, the lines around the unauthorized practice of law (UPL) are sufficiently blurry. Changing the regulatory framework for UPL in the US will likely follow a similar pattern to ride-sharing services. Enforcement will be slow, if at all, given the benefits of access to justice. When regulatory bodies understand the future state of what they are actually regulating, it will be political.

There is a saying that the US innovates and Europe regulates. In other words, the US tends to build and then regulate later. The experimentation with ABS in the US, coupled with UPL dynamics, is one reason for the significant investment in "legaltech" right now. Disruption is ripe, especially in the US markets. Some may be skeptical about regulators shying away from UPL enforcement; however, if we step back to see the bigger picture, the moves by consumers and legaltech investment are highly aligned politically with US policy. The world has entered a new industrial revolution, fueled by AI, amid high geopolitical tensions. The American-headquartered Magnificent Seven companies (Alphabet, Amazon, Apple, Meta, Microsoft, NVIDIA, Tesla) account for approximately 35 percent of the S&P 500's value. If these US companies were collectively a country, their GDP would exceed that of the European Union.[17] They have tremendous influence.

The US wants to win the AI Industrial Revolution, and its policies across administrations have been shaped to support that goal. Capital is being deployed at unprecedented levels to expand computing power, driving changes in construction, energy, and water policy to accommodate more data centers. Shifts in cybersecurity policy and steps to move semiconductor manufacturing onshore in the US and out of Taiwan are all intertwined.[18] OpenAI, Anthropic, and their Magnificent Seven partners will resist if they are brought into UPL enforcement actions. Given their alignment with US policy, it would be politically challenging to attempt to enforce at this stage, aside from egregious situations. There is more to lose than to win by enforcing UPL at this time. Regulatory enforcement runs afoul of politics and US policy.

The emergence of new roles and operating models

So, where is all this going? We are likely headed into a world where traditional boundaries fall and where there is greater specialization and new roles in law. There was a time when someone with a medical issue went to see a doctor or nurse. Now, there are many specialized medical roles, such as technicians who operate computed tomography scanners or X-ray equipment. In a similar vein, the application of AI and the rethinking of legal will create more specialized legal roles. Legal service providers have been trailblazers here, with roles in low-cost regions of the world and titles such as contract review specialist. In a world where legal workflows include AI, roles like legal engineers will be necessary for designing and maintaining them. Law firm information must be organized well for AI to use it, and there will be a greater need for data scientists and prompt engineers. With AI agents performing tasks, the roles around AI governance to protect confidential information and a firm's reputation will become essential.

AI-native law firms are at the forefront. This new class of law firm is rethinking the design of legal work from scratch, using AI as a foundational building block. Some are building using the tried-and-true partnership model with 100 percent law firm ownership, while others are embracing the legal services model and the advantages of ABS structures. There are big names in venture capital investing in firms that are starting with this philosophy, and dozens of firms are building out AI-based practices.[19,20,21] Several have over $100 million in financing and have attracted top talent from traditional firms.[22]

There are still questions about how large and how successful AI-native firms will be. Will they end up being a new breed of boutique firm? Will they be able to attract business away from large firms? Will their use of technology deliver objectively better outcomes for clients, or will it enable them to operate more efficiently? Will large firms acquire the successful AI-native law firms? There are many uncertainties, but one thing is clear: AI-native law firms will define the new standard of best practices, pushing traditional firms to change.

How traditional firms will adapt

Attorneys are trained to be cautious and question everything. They are paid to advise on risks, and relationships matter. Saving money on legal fees isn't the reason a client pays for a good M&A lawyer. When a complex acquisition is in play, the parties want the best attorneys who they can trust to get them the best deal. The goal is to get the deal done, and the relationship serves as a form of insurance that the deal won't go off the rails unnecessarily. Relationships are the moat that protects large firms, but they also enable legacy business practices that may not be efficient to persist.

While firms are moving to support multidisciplinary approaches and to collaborate across silos more frequently, there are still situations where client work starts from a blank canvas and does not effectively leverage the firm's collective learning and experience. Document-centric approaches to bespoke work product creation can linger as long as the client is willing to accept the billable hours charged. Caution is baked into the DNA of law firms, so change is typically deliberate and methodical, but losing out to competitors can change that very quickly.

Clients are increasingly interested not only in the outcome, but also in how the work gets done. If a client requests a task that can be completed manually, despite the fact that automation should be used, a firm can still deliver, but at lower profitability. However, when that same task is time-sensitive, the risk of losing the business to a more capable, mature firm is very real. It takes losing just one high-profile engagement to change a firm's behavior.

What if an AI-native law firm could demonstrate better outcomes for acquisition work? Could the use of AI during due diligence identify issues earlier and more comprehensively? Could the amount of money held back in escrow from the purchase price be materially reduced? When AI-native law firms or legal service providers deliver better outcomes for clients, traditional law firms will be forced to adapt.

The legal profession has long been driven by human capital, and attracting and retaining bright minds and talent have been central to the ongoing success of a firm. Technological advancements, such as typewriters, computers, word processing, and online legal research services, have notably enhanced the productivity of the legal profession. AI represents a tsunami of technological advancement that will further empower the human capital in law firms. Corporations and firms must continue to mature in technological expertise and in their use of AI tools to ensure they can attract and retain the talent they will need in the future. Firms will need to reevaluate staffing models and determine the optimal balance between practicing attorneys and an expanding set of other roles.

Technology will help make legal services more predictable. Productizing more legal services can reduce reliance on the billable hour, allowing firms to accommodate more staff who were once considered overhead.

Understanding the cost structure and profitability of matters will become clearer and more data-driven, empowering pricing specialists to price alternative fee arrangements (AFAs) that provide clients with predictability while also limiting downside risk for firms.

When calculators were introduced, some educators were concerned that students would undermine their learning of math concepts and that there would be overreliance on calculators, thereby impairing critical thinking. However, society benefits from the use of calculators, and educators have adapted. Similarly, new learning methods and staff training will need to be adjusted to the new realities of AI. Inexperienced associates will no longer learn by repetition, performing rote tasks over and over. Learning will need to consider AI chatbots and AI agents that perform work, much like a calculator performs math tasks. Partners can be cloned to create digital AI twins that are accessible at all hours to mentor new associates, quiz them, and coach along the way. In addition to new technology roles like legal engineers, the profession might consider more specialized certifications and more roles that do not require a full law degree.[23]

Designing the AI-enabled law firm

There has never been a more exciting period to be involved in the legal industry. The demand for legal services is strong. Potential solutions to enable greater access to justice exist. There is more investment in legal technology than ever seen before in the history of the profession. Law firms are facing pressure from many directions, and new categories of competition are gaining traction, such as legal service providers and AI-native law firms. The definition of the practice of law and of what constitutes a law firm is changing. Corporations are constantly motivated to drive for improvement. The changes they make ripple through the legal ecosystem.

A diverse talent pool and new roles are necessary to achieve the future state of the legal profession. The drudgery of endless hours of manual review is diminishing, allowing attorneys and others within firms to focus on more rewarding, cerebral activities. Like the medical profession, staffing needs to evolve, and specialized roles will emerge and become standardized.

Firms must increase their technological maturity to compete for talent. AI agents will perform more tasks, but will require staff for oversight. AI solutions like Claude Code can now create software without developers. Law firm staff will be able to quickly direct the creation of new applications that solve problems in firms that were once unimaginable.[24]

The justice system and the practice of law are central to the trust and confidence that businesses require to fuel economic growth, and it's also the hope and basis for civility in our societies. Generative AI has introduced tremendous opportunities in legal for people who are problem-solvers and looking for a higher purpose in their careers. Technology adoption always requires adjustments to people, processes, and data. For leaders in the legal profession, the need to understand and plan for new roles is urgent. Designing and planning for the AI-enabled, data-driven law firm starts now.

References

1 Hu K, "ChatGPT sets record for fastest-growing user base - analyst note", Reuters, 2 February 2023. See: https://www.reuters.com/technology/chatgpt-sets-record-fastest-growing-user-base-analyst-note-2023-02-01/.

2 Edwards B, "OpenAI upgrades GPT-3, stunning with rhyming poetry and lyrics", Ars Technica, 29 November 2022. See: https://arstechnica.com/information-technology/2022/11/openai-conquers-rhyming-poetry-with-new-gpt-3-update/.

3 Hatzius J, Briggs J, Kodnani D and Pierdomenico G, "The Potentially Large Effects of Artificial Intelligence on Economic Growth (Briggs/Kodnani)", Goldman Sachs, 26 March 2023. See: https://www.gspublishing.com/content/research/en/reports/2023/03/27/d64e052b-0f6e-45d7-967b-d7be35fabd16.html.

4 US Bureau of Economic Analysis, "Gross Domestic Product: Legal Services (5411) in the United States [USLEGALNGSP]", Federal Reserve Bank of St. Louis, 26 September 2025. See: https://fred.stlouisfed.org/series/USLEGALNGSP.

5 Judicial Council of California, *2025 Court Statistics Report: Statewide Caseload Trends, 2014–15 Through 2023–24*, 2025. See: https://courts.ca.gov/system/files/file/2025-court-statistics-report.pdf.

6 O'Keefe K, "Jack Newton on AI and the Latent Legal Market At ClioCon Hit Home", Real Lawyers Have Blogs, 6 November 2025. See: https://kevin.lexblog.com/2025/11/06/jack-newton-on-ai-and-the-latent-legal-market-at-cliocon-hit-home/.

7 Freedman R, "By looking elsewhere, companies send big law a message", Legal Dive, 7 October 2024. See: https://www.legaldive.com/news/BigHand-survey-law-firm-attrition-corporate-clients-lower-spend-DEI/729111/.

8 Zent M, "Why Choose an ALSP?", American Bar Association, 5 September 2023. See: https://www.americanbar.org/groups/law_practice/resources/law-technology-today/2023/why-choosean-alsp/.

9 Thomson Reuters Institute, The Center on Ethics and the Legal Profession at Georgetown Law and The Professional Service Firms (PSF) Group at Saïd Business School, University of Oxford, *Alternative Legal Services Providers 2025*, Thomson Reuters, 2025. See: https://www.thomsonreuters.com/en-us/posts/wp-content/uploads/sites/20/2025/01/ALSP-Report-2025.pdf.

10 *Ibid.* With $28 billion in 2023 and 18 percent growth, ALSPs will approach $50 billion in 2026.

11 American Bar Association, "Rule 5.4: Professional Independence of a Lawyer", 2026. See: https://www.americanbar.org/groups/professional_responsibility/publications/model_rules_of_professional_conduct/rule_5_4_professional_independence_of_a_lawyer/.

12 Anthony K, "Can You Own a Law Firm Without Being a Lawyer? - Non Lawyer Ownership Guide", Virtual Staffing, 18 November 2025. See: https://www.virtualstaffing.com/blog/can-you-own-a-law-firm-without-being-a-lawyer.

13 Legal Services Act 2007. See: https://www.legislation.gov.uk/ukpga/2007/29/contents.

14 "MSO" is terminology commonly used beyond the legal world to mean productized and predictable services, whereas the term "legal services" can be broader and apply to ad-hoc projects, overflow, and special tasks.

15 Tromans R, "PE Fund Merges 3 Groups into 1 for Opensity Giant", Artificial Lawyer, 17 February 2026. See: https://www.artificiallawyer.com/2026/02/17/pe-fund-merges-3-groups-into-1-for-opensity-giant/.

16 Perlo J and Yang A, "These people ditched lawyers for ChatGPT in court", NBC News, 8 October 2025. See: https://www.nbcnews.com/tech/innovation/ai-chatgpt-court-law-legal-lawyer-self-represent-pro-se-attorney-rcna230401.

17 Cingari P, "Magnificent Seven surpass EU GDP: Is this a tech bubble warning?", Yahoo Finance, 4 October 2025. See: https://finance.yahoo.com/news/magnificent-seven-surpass-eu-gdp-050117022.html?guccounter=1.

18 CHIPS Act of 2022, Pub. L. No. 117-167, 136 Stat. 1366 (2022).

19 PR Newswire, "Norm Ai Announces $50 Million Blackstone Investment, Launch of New AI-native Law Firm Norm Law", 20 November 2025. See: https://www.prnewswire.com/news-releases/norm-ai-announces-50-million-blackstone-investment-launch-of-new-ai-native-law-firm-norm-law-302621622.html.

20 Tromans R, "Y Combinator Picks 3 NewMods: General Legal, Arcline, LegalOS", Artificial Lawyer, 4 February 2026. See: https://www.artificiallawyer.com/2026/02/04/y-combinator-picks-3-newmods-general-legal-arcline-legalos/.

21 The AI Firm Index, "A Directory of AI-Native Law Firms", 2026. See: https://aifirmindex.com/.

22 Merken S, "Ex-Sidley Austin leader brings Big Law background to AI law firm", Reuters, 22 January 2026. See: https://www.reuters.com/legal/legalindustry/ex-sidley-austin-leader-brings-big-law-background-ai-law-firm-2026-01-22/.

23 An example of a certificate program for non-lawyers to be trained in the immigration process to guide those in need through the legal immigration process can be found here: https://www.villanova.edu/university/professional-studies/academics/professional-education/viista.html. It is a great example of understanding legal information and legal process without providing legal advice.

24 Mikeoss.com was recently released by an attorney in Singapore. The application is OpenSource, and firms can use it as the basis for creating their own equivalent to Harvey or Legora. See: Crutchfield K, "Ken Crutchfield: When Open Source Meets Legal — How MikeOSS Signals the End of Legal's Secret Sauce", LawSites, 8 May 2026. See: https://www.lawnext.com/2026/05/ken-crutchfield-when-open-source-meets-legal-how-mikeoss-signals-the-end-of-legals-secret-sauce.html.

Chapter 2: The legal engineer: Productizing legal work in the AI-enabled law firm

By Ali Chaudhry, senior legal engineer, Simmons & Simmons

In 1987, Richard Susskind introduced the concept of the legal knowledge engineer, a specialist who could work alongside lawyers, extract their expertise, and encode it into systems that others could use. The role was conceived as a back-office function, with the lawyer holding the domain knowledge and the engineer translating it into a form that technology could work with. What his original model did not account for was the kind of professional who would eventually end up performing that function.

I am one of those professionals. I originally studied law with the intention of qualifying as a lawyer, but I quickly found myself more interested in how legal work is structured and delivered than in the legal questions themselves. Combining that with a long-standing interest in technology and a drive to build things that improve how work gets done, legal engineering became the role that made sense for me.

That shift in direction coincided with a broader change in the legal market. From the 2010s onwards, firms and clients started taking technology more seriously, seeing it as something that could fundamentally change how legal services were designed and delivered, rather than simply as an internal efficiency tool. That created space for people who could sit between the legal and technical sides and make the two work together.

Generative artificial intelligence (genAI) accelerated all of this considerably. In my experience, the challenge in legal services today goes beyond what the law says. It is whether legal knowledge can actually be used at scale, consistently, across teams and organizations that are moving faster than traditional ways of working can keep up with. That requires a different kind of thinking from the one legal training produces.

For me, legal engineering has never felt like a departure from law – more a decision to engage with it from a different angle. I record time, price projects, and advise clients on AI adoption and value realization. The work is structured similarly to legal practice, even if the substance is different, and understanding how that came to be is what this chapter is about.

This chapter traces the lineage from Susskind's knowledge engineer to the legal engineer of today, and what the role involves in practice. Legal engineering is still young and genuinely varied, and what it looks like at one firm is not necessarily what it looks like at another. What follows is my best attempt to take stock of where the field is, drawing on my own practice and on the broader conversation happening across the profession. It is written from direct experience, rather than from the outside looking in, and that perspective shapes everything in it.

From knowledge engineer to legal engineer: How we got here

Open LinkedIn today and search for "legal engineer". You will find the title, or something close to it, across law firms, in-house legal teams, legal technology consultancies, and legal AI platforms like Harvey and Legora. It has become a recognizable career path; however, a decade ago, it barely existed by that name.

But what exactly is a legal engineer? The industry has not fully settled on a definition, and the way it has been described has changed as the role itself has developed. When Artificial Lawyer first attempted one in 2017, it described a legal engineer as "a person (lawyer or not) who improves a legal process or the delivery of legal services by leveraging legal technology and legal data".[1] That was a reasonable starting point for a field still finding its shape. Nearly a decade on, it captures the basic function, but understates what the work now involves. Alex Fortescue-Webb, who leads legal engineering at Legora, describes the strongest practitioners today as people who can "zoom into the detail of a specific workflow, then zoom out to see the broader organizational picture and design an adoption plan for the entire team, or even firm".[2] That framing reflects how the role has matured: A legal engineer today is less concerned with improving individual processes than with designing and owning the systems that allow legal knowledge to be used consistently and at scale. The role sits between legal practice and technical delivery and belongs fully to neither.

To understand why that role exists and why it looks the way it does, it helps to go back to where the idea came from. Susskind developed the concept of the legal knowledge engineer in his 1987 book *Expert Systems in Law*, drawing on research from his Oxford doctorate the previous year.[3] Expert systems are computer programs built to replicate the decision-making of a human expert in a defined domain. In medicine, such a system might help a clinician reach a diagnosis. In law, the goal was to capture legal rules and reasoning so that non-specialists could get answers without needing direct access to the lawyer whose knowledge it was based on.

The knowledge engineer's job was to draw out that expertise and represent it in a form a computer could work with. Susskind did this himself, collaborating with a leading authority on limitation periods in negligence law to develop what became the Latent Damage System, regarded at the time as the first commercially available expert system in English law. The role was a supporting one, in which the lawyer held the substantive knowledge and the knowledge engineer gave it structure. What connects that work to legal engineering today is the same underlying challenge of translation, taking what lives in a lawyer's head and turning it into something that can be used and scaled. The tools and techniques have changed considerably, but the challenge has not.

Before moving on, it is worth being precise about what Susskind did and did not define. When Artificial Lawyer asked him about it in 2017, he was clear that his two terms were specific. The legal knowledge engineer represented law in expert AI systems, and the legal information engineer, a term he discussed in his book *The Future of Law* in 1996, was concerned with structuring legal content for online delivery at a time when that was only beginning to emerge.[4] He acknowledged that his uses "may have been more specific" than the broader term that eventually took hold.[5] As this section will show, the field developed through practitioners doing the work and gradually naming what they were doing, building on his ideas in ways he had not anticipated.

By the time Susskind published *Tomorrow's Lawyers* in 2013, his thinking had moved on. The book was aimed at practitioners and aspiring lawyers, rather than academics. What had changed was not the underlying concept, but the scale at which he now believed it would be needed. In the 1980s, the role was a specialist function supporting a handful of complex projects. By 2013, advances in cloud computing and increasingly accessible software had made it possible to build and deploy legal systems at a scale and cost that had not previously existed. Legal services were also under growing commercial pressure to change how they delivered value. Those forces together suggested the market would need a new class of professional operating across firms and alongside clients.[6] What that professional would look like, and where they would come from, was a question the field would answer for itself.

In practice, that shift was already under way. By around 2014, at least one major law firm was using "legal knowledge engineer" as an operational job title. Pinsent Masons had invested early in document automation and was expanding into process mapping and AI development. As that work grew, the firm found itself with people whose roles could not be adequately described by existing job titles. They were not IT staff, whose work was maintaining systems rather than designing legal solutions. They were not knowledge lawyers, whose focus was capturing expertise in written form. The work they were doing required them to understand legal processes well enough to design systems around them, and to understand technology well enough to make those systems work. The closest available vocabulary was Susskind's, and the firm used it.[7] It is worth mentioning that Catherine Bamford, who had led much of that work, went on to build an independent consultancy doing the same thing for other clients. Looking back, this highlighted that the market was willing to pay for this kind of work on its own terms. Legal engineering was not just something a progressive firm had created internally; it was something clients valued enough to commission as a service in its own right.

By 2016, the conversation had become more public. Stuart Barr, formerly chief product and strategy officer at HighQ, published "The Rise of the Legal Engineer", making the case that the legal industry had reached a tipping point.[8] Barr argued that the legal engineer was the interface between legal and technology expertise, someone who understood both sides well enough to identify where the real problems were and design solutions that neither side could reach alone. He observed that practitioners typically arrived at the role from one of two directions – from law into technology or the other way around – but that deep understanding of both was the defining characteristic either way. Barr's piece gave shared language to something that had been happening across organizations without a common name, which was a significant milestone in the field in retrospect.

Drew Winlaw, then in the process of co-founding Wavelength.law, read the piece and wrote a response describing what the term had meant to him personally. He had started his working life in Australia in manufacturing, later training and practicing as a commercial technology lawyer in the UK, and found the processes inside law firms and legal teams, in his own words, "horrifying".[9] However, moving between those worlds gave him a set of skills to fix many of the issues he encountered. Barr's piece crystallized something for Winlaw: "Identifying myself as a legal engineer was something of an epiphany," he wrote.[10] "I recognized many of the new law firm roles predicted" by Richard Susskind. In time I gravitated away from practicing as a lawyer towards troubleshooting and fixing processes for legal teams."[11] His response made clear that this experience was not unusual. There were practitioners across the profession who had arrived at the same place by different routes without realizing others had too. Naming the role made it possible to find each other, and the field began to take shape from that point.

What followed was the first attempt to give legal engineering a formal professional structure. Wavelength, which Winlaw co-founded with Peter Lee in 2016, operated under authorization from the Solicitors Regulation Authority (SRA) as a legal practice, rather than a technology consultancy. That distinction made the business stand out significantly. SRA authorization placed Wavelength under the same professional regulatory framework as any law firm, with duties to clients, professional indemnity requirements, and accountability to a regulatory body that a technology consultancy does not carry. By operating as a regulated legal practice, Wavelength was making a specific claim about what kind of service legal engineering was. Its legal engineers were fee-earners who billed clients directly for their work, rather than being absorbed into the overhead of a broader engagement, and that positioned legal engineering as something clients valued enough to pay for in its own right.

When Simmons and Simmons acquired Wavelength in 2019, it confirmed that idea at scale.[12] Jeremy Hoyland, the firm's managing partner at the time, was direct about the reasoning:

> *We approached Wavelength because we wanted to provide a better offering for our clients. All the big firms have been struggling with this area. Wavelength has a lot of people who can help with this, and it would have been hard to grow such a capability organically.*[13]

That last point is the significant one. A firm of Simmons' size and resource had concluded that building legal engineering capability from within was not a reliable path. The professionals who could do this work developed through years of experience at the intersection of legal and technical practice, and that kind of experience cannot be replicated by restructuring a job title or running a training program.

The legal engineer of today did not arrive through the back-office technical function Susskind's earlier work described. It came from the client-facing world of legal practice, and through people who came from the legal side with enough technical curiosity to develop genuine fluency in both directions. A legal engineer who started in law brings an understanding of how legal work feels from the inside, and that understanding cannot be acquired from a brief or a training course. It is the foundation on which everything else the role requires is built.

One practical consequence of the field developing this way is that the terminology has never standardized. Firms use different titles for roles that overlap considerably, and that can create problems. A firm advertising for a legal technologist when it actually needs a legal engineer may attract the wrong person. A practitioner building a career in the field may find themselves miscategorized, simply because the title they hold at one firm means something different at another. In broad terms, the legal technologist tends to sit closest to a technology implementation function, configuring platforms and training teams on new systems. The legal process engineer tends to focus on workflow design and process improvement. The legal knowledge engineer, in Susskind's original sense, represents legal logic in systems so it can be applied consistently at scale. The legal engineer, as the term is most commonly used today, tends to span all of these, with the balance shifting depending on what the firm or client needs.

However, what these roles share matters more than the differences their titles imply. They are all concerned with the same translation function Susskind originally identified: taking legal expertise and giving it a form that technology can work with and that people can use. What distinguishes the best legal engineers from that original back-office conception is the capacity to exercise independent professional judgment. A legal engineer advising on whether a process should be automated at all, or whether the proposed technical approach is right for this context, is making a professional call that requires credibility with both the legal team and the technical team simultaneously. That credibility only comes when the legal engineer genuinely understands both worlds well enough to be trusted by specialists on both sides, rather than knowing a little about each without going deep enough to be useful when it matters.

Getting to that point, as this section has tried to show, took the better part of four decades. It started with an academic concept, moved through quiet adoption inside law firms, surfaced in public conversations in the mid-2010s and eventually attracted the kind of institutional investment that signals a field has arrived. Legal engineering is still young and the terminology is still unsettled, but the role is real, it is in demand and it is not going away.

What the role actually involves

Having covered the history and terminology, the next area to approach is what the role entails. Interestingly, the activity that most defines a legal engineer's working life is not actually building anything. It is translation, converting the way one group of highly trained experts thinks about a problem into terms that a completely different group of highly trained experts can act on. Legal engineers spend a significant part of their time in the space between lawyers and technologists, and making that conversation work is harder than most people expect.

The difficulty starts with the fact that the two sides are not just using different vocabulary; they have been trained to value different things. A data scientist or solutions architect approaches a problem with an instinct towards technical elegance, favoring something architecturally clean and scalable well beyond what the immediate use case requires. That instinct is not inherently wrong, as it comes from years of working in environments where building something robust from the start saves enormous pain later. In a technology company building infrastructure for millions of users, that orientation makes perfect sense. In a law firm where a senior associate needs to complete a contract review at 11pm before a completion deadline, it is a different story. Legal practice operates under acute time pressure and high levels of risk aversion, with stakeholder dynamics that technical teams without direct legal experience tend to underestimate. A system that is technically impressive but too cumbersome to use under those conditions has not solved the problem; it has created a different one. The legal engineer's job is to prevent that from happening.

Doing that credibly requires enough technical understanding to evaluate whether a proposed approach is proportionate to the problem. You do not need to be able to build it, and the suggestion that legally trained people should learn to code misses the point entirely. Technical specialists have trained hard to perform the work they do, just as lawyers have, and the idea that either can simply pick up the other's core skills alongside their day job understates both professions. What a legal engineer actually needs is a working understanding of what the technology can do reliably; where it tends to fail; and what the real trade-offs are between a more sophisticated approach and one that is simpler but more likely to be used. That understanding develops through sustained exposure and genuine curiosity, rather than through formal technical training. It is what separates a legal engineer from a capable lawyer who has developed an interest in technology.

The challenge runs in both directions, however. Translating a technical approach into something a legal team can properly evaluate is equally demanding. Lawyers are trained to work towards conclusions, as opposed to assessing the design of systems. When a legal team is presented with a solution design, they can struggle to distinguish between what is technically feasible, what is genuinely achievable within the project constraints, and what has been proposed, because it happens to be the path of least resistance for the developers. A legal engineer must be able to explain the relevant technical concepts clearly enough for non-technical stakeholders to make real decisions, without oversimplifying in ways that mislead or getting lost in detail that does not help anyone. That is a communication skill as much as a technical one, and it takes time to develop.

Much of the most important work happens before anything is built. Gathering requirements from lawyers and business stakeholders is a skilled activity that is consistently underestimated. The reason people rarely describe the right problem is structural. Lawyers are trained to identify issues and reach conclusions, not to articulate the underlying process that needs to change. What comes across as a request for a tool is often a symptom of something deeper that the tool alone will not fix. A legal engineer must listen carefully enough to hear what is actually being asked, test the assumptions underlying it, and turn a loosely articulated need into something specific enough to build from. The business requirements or solution design that comes out of that process is not administrative work; it is the foundation on which the quality of everything that follows depends.

Process mapping sits in the same space. For readers less familiar with the term, process mapping means visualizing how work moves through an organization step by step, identifying where decisions are made, where knowledge lives only in one person's head, and where a process could be systematized. It requires legal literacy to do properly. Someone who does not understand the legal workflow will draw a map that misses the points where human judgment is genuinely irreplaceable and overstates where automation will work. The result is a build that looks efficient on paper and breaks down in practice.

From there, the work moves into design and build. This can involve configuring platforms like HighQ, which is used primarily for client collaboration, matter management, and portal solutions, or ContractExpress, which automates document generation. It involves designing the instructions that govern how large language models (LLMs) behave within a specific legal task

– work that is commonly called prompt engineering, but is arguably closer to knowledge engineering in a legal context. The goal is to capture the expertise of a senior practitioner in enough structured detail that an AI system can apply it reliably without that practitioner being present. The build stage also increasingly involves data pipelines that process large volumes of legal content into structured outputs, and lightweight prototyping to test whether an approach is viable before committing to a full build. In my experience, being willing to experiment and comfortable being wrong early tends to produce better outcomes than trying to specify everything upfront, because real-world testing surfaces problems that no amount of planning can anticipate.

The common thread is a project management dimension that the role does not always get enough credit for. A legal engineer on a substantial engagement is holding the requirements, the solution design, the stakeholder relationships, and the delivery timeline simultaneously. Getting all of that right is what creates the conditions for the technical work to be delivered at all. A technically sound solution that lands in an organization without adequate preparation or stakeholder buy-in will not be adopted, and an unadopted solution has not delivered much value.

The outputs of all this work vary considerably, but they reflect a consistent underlying purpose, which is making legal expertise more usable at scale. They include automated document assembly workflows; contract templates with embedded clause logic; playbooks that capture a firm's negotiating positions; tools that allow clients to work through a structured process without requiring lawyer time at every step; and prompt libraries that put the judgment of a senior practitioner in the hands of the whole team. Each of these represents the same underlying achievement. Legal knowledge that previously lived in one person's head, or in a document that nobody could find, has been given a form that the organization can actually use.

The range of activities described in this section might make legal engineering sound like a collection of different jobs loosely grouped under one title. In a sense, it is, but what holds it together is the ability to move between the legal and technical worlds with enough fluency to be genuinely useful in both, and to exercise the kind of judgment that neither side could apply on its own.

Productizing legal services

One of the things that became clear to me relatively quickly in my career is that the translation work described in the previous section is not just about individual tools or projects. Done well and at scale, it changes the nature of what a firm can offer its clients. That is what this section is about.

Consider a legal team responsible for keeping pace with a fast-moving regulatory landscape. Every time something changes, the team needs to understand the implications, work out what action is required, and build something internally that can be tracked over time. If this task is approached manually, the process is slow. By the time one set of changes has been worked through, more have arrived, and the team is already behind.

Now consider an alternative. Instead of working through each change manually, the team receives a structured output mapping every relevant obligation, summarizing what it requires, and designed in such a way that the document is updated as the position evolves. The underlying legal analysis is equivalent in quality to a manual review. The difference is in how it is delivered and how useful it is to the people who receive it.

That is what productization means in the context of legal services: it is the process of taking legal work that was previously delivered as one-off bespoke advice and turning it into something that can be structured and delivered repeatedly. The distinction is important, because it changes the nature of the value a firm can provide. A one-off advice note is useful once, but a well-designed tool built on the same expertise continues to be useful as the law and the client's circumstances evolve.

Not every piece of legal work can be treated this way, however, and understanding why is as key as understanding the opportunity. Most legal work contains two distinct layers. The first is genuine judgment: the analysis that depends on the specific facts of a matter, the client's circumstances, and the context they are operating in. This layer is different on every instruction, and trying to standardize it means removing the thing that makes it valuable. The second layer is the underlying analytical framework: the logical steps from input to output; the structure of the analysis that tends to remain consistent, even when the content varies entirely from one matter to the next. Productization works on the second layer. It builds infrastructure around the repeatable parts of a process so that lawyer time and judgment can be reserved for the parts that genuinely require them.

Take legislative comparison as an example. When a piece of legislation is amended or replaced, legal teams need to understand what has changed and what it means for them. If approached manually, that involves reading two versions of the law carefully, identifying the differences and assessing their significance. It is time-consuming work, but the underlying analytical logic is the same, regardless of which law is being compared. A legal engineer can build a structured process around that logic, with an LLM handling the initial comparison and lawyers reviewing the output before it reaches whoever needs it. What would previously have taken considerable manual time can be delivered faster, in a form that is immediately usable, rather than requiring further processing.

Working out which pieces of legal work are genuinely product-ready requires honest assessment. Firms that get this wrong tend to make one of two mistakes. The first is trying to productize work where the bespoke judgment layer is too thick: where the lawyer's involvement is required at every stage, and systematizing the repeatable parts saves very little time. The product looks plausible on paper, but does not deliver meaningful efficiency because it cannot reduce the lawyer time required. The second mistake is failing to productize work that is clearly ready: where the logic is consistent and the volume is high, but the investment has not been made because the commercial pressure has not yet become acute enough. The legal engineer's role in both cases is to assess the work honestly and make the case to the people who need to commission it.

There is a further difficulty that even well-designed products may encounter. In practice, clients could have requirements the original product was not designed to handle, and the instinct on both sides is to accommodate them. A tool designed to do a specific job gets asked to do something slightly different, and then something else. Each request is reasonable in isolation but, cumulatively, they push what started as a repeatable product back into bespoke territory. The infrastructure is still there, but the delivery has drifted into something that is neither scalable nor efficient. This is one of the genuine structural reasons why productizing legal services is harder than it looks and requires ongoing discipline, rather than a one-time design exercise. GenAI has made the problem somewhat more manageable, because language models can often accommodate variation that hard-coded rule systems cannot. However, the tendency for scope to creep does not disappear.

Once a piece of work has been identified as a candidate, the question of what form the delivery should take depends on the nature of the work and what the client needs. A self-service tool lets the client run the process without requiring real-time lawyer involvement. A managed service keeps the firm involved operationally, running the process on the client's behalf. Both have merit and both have limitations, and the right choice is shaped by data governance questions; the client's technical environment; and how the commercial relationship is structured. A legal engineer navigating these choices must understand all of those dimensions, which is why the role cannot sit entirely on either the legal or the technical side.

Whatever form the product takes, the quality requirement does not change. A productized legal service that delivers outputs a lawyer would not stand behind is not worth having. The review processes that sit between the automated output and the client are not transitional arrangements to be removed once the system has been running for a while; rather, they are what makes the output trustworthy. Firms that treat that review layer as overhead to be eliminated tend to find out why it existed at some point after it has gone.

What productization really represents is legal engineering operating at its most ambitious. Building a single tool is one thing; designing a service that can be delivered repeatedly, at quality, at scale, in a way that keeps adapting as the law changes, is considerably harder. It is also where the most interesting and durable work happens.

How legal engineers work with lawyers and IT

The work described in the previous section does not happen in isolation. Legal engineers operate within organizations that have their own structures, cultures, and constraints, and how the function is set up inside a firm shapes what it can deliver. That is worth spending some time on, because getting it wrong is likely to be more common than it should be.

Ask ten law firms how they have structured their legal engineering function, and you will get ten different answers. Some have built central teams serving the whole firm as an internal resource. Others have embedded legal engineers within specific practice groups, sitting alongside the lawyers who do the work. Many have tried both at different points and drawn different conclusions. Neither of these models is inherently right or wrong in my opinion – I have experienced both sides.

A central team gives legal engineers broad exposure. They encounter different practice areas, types of client work, and ways of thinking about problems, which builds a kind of cross-firm pattern recognition that a more narrowly focused role cannot provide. However, the problem with this approach is visibility. In a large firm, a central team can become invisible to the people who most need it. Partners who already understand what legal engineering is will seek the team out. Those who do not will not, which is precisely the wrong way around. Without active internal presence and a clear route for people to engage with the function, a central team tends to become reactive, working on whatever comes through the door, rather than on the problems that would deliver the most value.

Practice embedding solves the visibility problem, but creates a different one. A legal engineer sitting within a practice group becomes a genuine part of that team. They understand its specific workflows and work at the same pace and under the same pressures as the lawyers around them. That proximity builds trust in a way that a central function cannot easily replicate. The risk here is narrowness as, without deliberate coordination across the firm, different practice groups end up solving the same problems, independently accumulating learning that never reaches anyone else.

The practical implication is that the operating model matters less than the mechanisms connecting it to the rest of the firm. A well-designed intake process and a structured relationship with IT will make either model work better. The absence of those things will undermine either.

On intake, the instinct of many legal engineers early in their careers is to say "yes" to everything, and I have certainly been guilty of that. A partner asks for a tool, and you build it. A client has an interesting problem, and you solve it. That instinct is understandable, and it is often what the people around them want. The problem is that, without discipline around intake, a legal engineering function fills up with low-priority requests and never accumulates the compound knowledge that makes it genuinely effective over time. Lawyers manage their own intake carefully: they take instructions, clarify scope, and push back when a request is underdeveloped. A legal engineer who does not apply the same discipline will consistently find themselves building things that solve the wrong problem or solving the right problem in a way that cannot be reused.

When a legal engineer resists the urge to treat every request as a fresh challenge, they start to build institutional memory. The work performed on one matter becomes the foundation for the next. Prompts and workflow designs developed the first time can be refined and reused and eventually systematized into something the firm can rely on. What started as bespoke becomes repeatable. That is the same underlying logic as productization applied to the legal engineer's own practice, and the firms that benefit most from their legal engineering capability are usually the ones where this kind of accumulation has been allowed to happen deliberately, rather than by accident.

The governance of what gets built matters as much as the design, as a deployed solution is not finished. When the law changes or the platform it runs on is updated, someone must assess the impact and decide how to respond. When ownership is unclear, those moments tend to be handled poorly. Legal engineers who own a solution entirely may not have the technical capability to update it safely. IT teams that own it without legal engineering involvement may not understand what a legal change means for how the solution should behave. What works is shared ownership with clearly defined responsibilities. Legal engineers and the relevant legal teams assess what any change means for the solution's logic and outputs, while IT manages the platform and ensures changes are deployed safely. That requires an ongoing working relationship between the two sides, rather than a handover at the point of build.

That relationship needs to start early. IT need to be involved at the beginning of any legal engineering project, as opposed to after the design has been agreed. A firm's technical environment shapes what is buildable, and the constraints it imposes on data governance, platform integration, and deployment cannot be retrofitted onto a design that was produced without taking them into account. A legal engineer who discovers at deployment that the technical environment cannot support what has been designed has wasted time on both sides.

How a legal engineering function is structured, how it manages intake, and how it works with IT are not secondary concerns – they are the conditions under which everything else either works or does not. The most technically capable legal engineer in the wrong structure, without the right relationships or the right governance around what they build, will consistently underdeliver. Getting the operating environment right is as much a part of the job as the engineering itself.

Skills, backgrounds, and what firms are looking for

Everything discussed so far – the translation work, the productization, the operating models – ultimately comes down to people. What kind of person does legal engineering well? Where do they come from, and what are firms actually looking for when they hire them? These are questions the field has been working out in practice, and the answers are still evolving.

There is no single path into legal engineering. That is not a temporary feature of a young field that will eventually standardize. It reflects what the role actually requires, which is a blend of legal understanding and technical curiosity that can be developed from genuinely different starting points.

People who come from legal practice bring something that is difficult to acquire any other way. It is an instinctive feel for how legal work operates in practice: the pace, the risk aversion, and the way decisions get made under pressure. That grounding makes it considerably easier to build things that lawyers will use, and to push back credibly when a proposed solution does not fit the conditions of real practice. The limitation is that lawyers who move into legal engineering can sometimes struggle with the technical dimension – not because they are incapable of developing it, but because legal training does not naturally produce the kind of systems thinking that engineering requires.

People who come from legal technology vendors may arrive with deep platform knowledge and a good sense of what technology can and cannot do in a legal context. What they sometimes lack is the domain knowledge that only comes from being inside legal practice, rather than serving it from the outside. That gap is real and shows in the work. A legal engineer who has never worked closely alongside lawyers on live matters will often design solutions that make sense technically and miss how a legal team will behave when using them.

People from legal operations backgrounds are often closer to the legal engineering mindset than they realize. Their focus on process improvement and workflow design maps nicely onto what legal engineers do. The distinction tends to be on the build side. Legal operations professionals manage and improve existing processes, while legal engineers design and build the systems those processes run on.

A smaller but rising number of legal engineers come from genuinely technical backgrounds and build their legal domain knowledge through sustained exposure to the profession. This route can produce exceptional practitioners, although it takes longer and requires a deliberate effort to understand legal work from the inside, which technical training alone does not provide.

What all of these routes share, in the people who do the work well, is harder to describe than any background or skillset. The best legal engineers think in systems, in a practical, rather than abstract, sense. When they encounter a problem, their first response is to understand its shape before proposing a solution. They ask who owns it, what the workflow looks like, and what has been tried before. That analytical patience is not produced by legal or technical training; it is a disposition, and it consistently distinguishes people who are genuinely effective in this role from those who are merely technically qualified for it. Someone without it tends to produce solutions that are technically sound but wrong, because the problem they solved was not the problem that existed.

What firms look for has become clearer as the field has matured. Legal domain knowledge and an understanding of how lawyers work day-to-day sit at the top of most hiring criteria, alongside some working knowledge of genAI and how it applies in practice. The ability to communicate across different audiences matters considerably. Explaining technical concepts to lawyers and translating legal requirements into something precise enough for a developer to act on are both things the role demands, and neither comes naturally to everyone. Project management ability is helpful too, but it is not the most important quality. A legal engineer on a substantial engagement may typically coordinate multiple workstreams while managing relationships across legal and technical teams simultaneously; when any of that slips, the consequences can cascade.

What has also become clearer is that what a firm needs from a legal engineer varies considerably depending on what it is trying to do. A firm focused primarily on AI adoption needs someone who can design training and help lawyers build productive working habits around new tools. A firm building client-facing products needs someone who can gather requirements, design systems, and work with developers through a build and test cycle. These are recognizably the same kind of professional, although the emphasis differs, and firms that are not precise about what they need are likely to discover the mismatch after they have hired.

Unsurprisingly, legal engineer career trajectories are still being written. The field is young enough that there is no settled picture of where a legal engineer goes after a decade of sustained practice. What is clear is that the skills the role develops are becoming more valuable as AI reshapes legal services. Some legal engineers could move into senior leadership roles within firms, shaping technology and innovation strategy at a firm-wide level. Others could move to clients, where some in-house legal teams are increasingly looking to build their own engineering capability. The technology companies building the platforms legal engineers work with every day are also an increasingly attractive destination because a practitioner's perspective on what works in a legal context may be scarcer there.

For anyone who has spent serious time in this role, a return to work that sits entirely on one side of the legal–technical divide probably becomes difficult to imagine. Once you have built a practice at the intersection of those two worlds, operating within the constraints of either one alone is a significant narrowing. That is not an argument for why everyone should become a legal engineer; it is an observation about what the work does to the people who do it well.

Conclusion

As this chapter has shown, legal engineering is a young discipline; in some ways, that is still visible. The terminology is unsettled, the career paths are still being written, and firms are still working out how to get the most from the function. That is not a criticism – it is an honest description of where a field is when it has gone from an academic concept to a recognizable professional practice in a decade, and getting to this point has required more than most people realize.

What this chapter has tried to demonstrate is what the role actually is and what it requires. A legal engineer is not necessarily a lawyer who has developed an interest in technology or a technologist who has picked up enough legal context to sound credible in legal conversations. The role is something more specific than either of those descriptions allows. It requires someone who has built genuine fluency in both directions and who can exercise independent judgment about where the two worlds need to meet. That capacity does not emerge from training programs or job title changes. It develops through sustained experience at the intersection of the two professions, and this is why legal engineering is a professional identity, rather than a job description.

The conditions under which that identity can flourish matter considerably, and this is something firms may not always get right. A legal engineer who is given real responsibility, integrated properly with legal and technical teams, and involved in decisions about what gets built will perform work that is genuinely valuable. A legal engineer hired into a structure that treats the role as a support function, without the authority to push back on poor solutions or the access the work requires, will struggle to deliver that value, regardless of how capable they are. My experience shows that the role must be embedded in the work, rather than positioned at a distance from it.

I came to legal engineering because I was more interested in how legal services are produced than in any individual piece of legal work, and because the most interesting problems I could see in the profession sat at the intersection of law and technology, rather than within either discipline alone. That has not changed – if anything, the intersection has become more consequential as the tools have become more powerful. Deciding when AI is the right answer, assessing what makes a piece of legal work genuinely product-ready, or figuring out how to build something that will be trusted and used – these conundrums require a greater degree of judgment now than they did five years ago, and they are harder to get right. That is also what makes them more worth working on.

The legal engineer is a professional identity to be chosen. The field is young enough that the choice still feels like a real one. The firms and practitioners who understand that will be better placed for what comes next.

References

1 Tromans R, "Lawyer to Trademark 'Legal Engineer', But Who Invented the Term?", Artificial Lawyer, 7 December 2017. See: https://www.artificiallawyer.com/2017/12/07/lawyer-to-trademark-legal-engineer-but-who-invented-the-term/.

2 Fortescue-Webb A, "The Rise of the Legal Engineer: Making AI Work in Law", Legora, 4 September 2025. See: https://legora.com/blog/the-rise-of-the-legal-engineer-making-ai-work-in-law.

3 Tromans R, "Lawyer to Trademark 'Legal Engineer', But Who Invented the Term?", *Artificial Lawyer*, 7 December 2017. See: https://www.artificiallawyer.com/2017/12/07/lawyer-to-trademark-legal-engineer-but-who-invented-the-term/.

4 *Ibid.*

5 *Ibid.*

6 Susskind R, *Tomorrow's Lawyers* (2nd edn), Oxford: Oxford University Press; 2017: 135.

7 Tromans R, "Lawyer to Trademark 'Legal Engineer', But Who Invented the Term?", *Artificial Lawyer*, 7 December 2017. See: https://www.artificiallawyer.com/2017/12/07/lawyer-to-trademark-legal-engineer-but-who-invented-the-term/.

8 Barr S, "The Rise of the Legal Engineer", Lexology, 27 July 2016. See: https://www.lexology.com/library/detail.aspx?g=f8d9bb92-3779-4bc2-9f1b-7354d416acb1.

9 Winlaw D, "Are You a Legal Engineer?", LinkedIn, 31 August 2016. See: https://www.linkedin.com/pulse/you-legal-engineer-drew-winlaw.

10 *Ibid.*

11 *Ibid.*

12 Simmons & Simmons, "We've acquired legal engineering firm Wavelength", 23 July 2019. See: https://www.simmons-simmons.com/about-us/news/230719-simmons-and-simmons-acquires-legal-engineering-firm-wavelength.

13 Tromans R, "Wavelength + Simmons & Simmons Combination: News Analysis", *Artificial Lawyer*, 24 July 2019. See: https://www.artificiallawyer.com/2019/07/24/wavelength-simmons-simmons-combination-news-analysis/.

Chapter 3:
Legal data scientists and analytics leaders: The rise of legal intelligence

By Matthew J. Dunne, AI solutions lead, K&L Gates LLP

Innovation at law firms goes through cycles. Not every new way of thinking and doing meets with the same amount of success. Lessons are learned; new ideas germinate and grow; and, sometimes, they grow and mature in other industries, and law firms adopt them.

This metaphor can be extended further. Think of that flowering seed as a particular discipline, called data science. Can it grow in the soil that is the legal industry? How must it change and adapt? What does it yield in the harvest? In this chapter, we shall attempt to answer these questions. It will attempt to offer practical guidance as to how data science is being used and implemented at law firms, although the scope of application is so wide and deep that we can hardly be comprehensive.

First, we shall put data science, and data scientists, in the context of other, similar professionals you would find at a law firm. We will then explore what that work looks like in its actual delivery, including both its strengths and its limitations. After that, we will address governance, an integral part of the process for law firms with significant upstream and downstream effects. Finally, we will elaborate on earlier topics and bring everything together in a discussion of value to the organization.

What is a data scientist?

To understand how data science can take root in legal practice, we must first define what a data scientist actually does. The best, and most common, way of understanding it is to imagine a Venn diagram containing three circles representing coding, statistics, and business. Data science is where all three overlap. This is different from traditional business intelligence (BI) or analytics, which is relatively less dependent on coding and statistics. A BI specialist can certainly understand and use certain models, such as linear regression, but not at the same level as a data scientist.

Similarly, there is a distinction between data science and data engineering.

The former is more a consumer of the data for the purpose of completing a deeper analysis; the latter is responsible for getting where it needs to be in a reliable and accurate way. In practice, there is a great deal of overlap in these functions, with the same person or group filling both roles.

In the context of law firms and legal departments, the most important distinction is probably between data scientists and *legal* engineers. Legal engineers are more embedded in the lawyers' process so that they can understand and re-engineer it, most likely with generative artificial intelligence (AI). Data scientists are usually not embedded with attorneys, although there are instances of them working on client matters. Instead, data scientists analyze the work from somewhat of a distance. Their projects are more empirical and less customized. Data scientists are not hired to work with only part of the organization – the investments in databases, architecture, and engineering are, necessarily comprehensive to the whole organization, both practically and economically. A data scientist will likely know more about AI – even generative AI – than a legal engineer. The math, the statistics, and the code are a core part of the curriculum, although – in practice and depending on the scope of what a legal engineer's duties are – this may not matter much.

Unless an organization is developing its own tools, there will be limited opportunity for this extra AI knowledge to come into play. The organization has the tools that it has, and data scientists have little advantage in learning the intricacies of software features or in writing prompts tailored to a particular scenario compared to legal engineers. The real advantage data scientists have is a grounding in computational thinking, where solutions can be pieced together when the roadblock is technical, involving issues such as data structures or algorithms. With that foundation in mind, we turn to how data scientists operate within legal delivery.

Data in legal delivery

Why does the legal industry employ data scientists

The ability to analyze and process structured and unstructured data is rapidly becoming essential to modern legal work. It touches areas as diverse as:

- Litigation analytics;
- Contract analysis;
- eDiscovery;
- Compliance monitoring; and
- Legal operations, pricing, and profitability.

This is to say nothing of generative AI, which has perhaps become the most predominant use case in recent years.

It may be something of an oversimplification, but – in the past – producers and consumers of legal services were content if bills went out and the client felt it was getting value for money. Further analysis or inquiry was not practical given the state of technology. That is no longer the case.

Everyone agrees there is some insight or advantage to be gained from parsing the available datasets, but the required skillset is not traditionally part of law firms or legal departments. The value proposition of data scientists is that they can ensure there is a rigorous, quantitative basis behind the analysis of past data, which makes it reliable for informing future action.

This is a relatively recent phenomenon, with several independent forces responsible for its inception. The first is increased pressure from clients to reduce costs. The second is advances in AI and natural language processing that excite the imagination and keep the attention of stakeholders. The third is all the groundwork that has been done around data infrastructure, thus enabling data scientists to have something to work with.

Before we move onto the next section, let us take a brief diversion to explore the relationship between data scientists and generative AI. The standard data science curriculum will cover statistics, modelling, machine learning, neural networks, and natural language processing (NLP). Generative AI and large language models (LLMs) are a relatively recent development. They are somewhat separate from traditional data science, although they draw from much the same foundation. The point is that a data scientist and a generative AI specialist are not necessarily the same thing. However, the former is in a very good position to become the latter.

In delivery

It would be helpful to go over some examples of projects a data scientist might work on in the legal field. These are not meant to be comprehensive, but should give a good idea on the breadth of possible applications for data science skills.

Example #1: Building a HR chatbot

All sufficiently large organizations will have a large inflow of questions from employees on HR matters. The answers to these questions exist in documents, probably available through an intranet, but finding them is just cumbersome enough that most people resort to emailing someone in HR. Responding to these emails is probably not the best use of the HR professional's time. The solution: build a retrieval augmented generation-based (RAG) chatbot, preferably using the tools already available, that can answer these basic questions, based on a pre-existing set of documents.

Example #2: Deploying NLP-based models

Say there is a dashboard to track utilization within a practice group. It draws on data from the firm's system. There is a variable that the system does not capture, because it would be too burdensome to do so – with any accuracy, at least. An example might be task codes, as delineated by the American Bar Association's Uniform Task-Based Management System (UTMBS).[1] Having this information, even if imputed, would be extremely helpful for the purpose of the dashboard. The solution: build a model that takes time entries and predicts a task code from them, and deploy it to the dashboard to automatically update with new data.

The common thread with these examples is that a data scientist understands the problem; correctly identifies what success looks like; maps the proper quantitative and analytical techniques onto the data at hand; and produces a deliverable.

What data can and cannot do

It is important to clarify what data science can and cannot do in the legal context. There are commonly recognized types of data analytics (a good enough synonym for data science). These include:

- Descriptive analytics (explain what happened);
- Diagnostic analytics (explain why it happened);
- Predictive analytics (forecast what will happen); and
- Prescriptive analytics (recommend an action).

The limits of prediction

Some types of analytics are more common in the legal industry than others. "Prediction" is a loaded term that is worth close examination. There are very few instances of true predictive modelling, because there are not many scenarios in which true probabilistic calculations come into play. In my personal experience, predictive analytics in legal tend to be in classification (discrete categories or labels), rather than regression (continuous, numerical values). Examples of these include classification by matter type or predicting task code based on time entry narrative. These have obvious applications for resource management between firm and client.

The limits of prediction are easiest to grasp in the context of litigation. It might be a gamble in the colloquial sense, but games of chance can be modelled out quantitatively. You know there is a one in six chance for any value on the throw of a die. That is not the same for a trial outcome: you might have data that outline a certain percentage of times a certain type of motion is successful in a certain type of case, but that only tells you so much, because all cases are different. In theory, one could extract features from many cases and fit a model that performs well in minimizing error in a classic train–test split. However, there is a reason lawyers are famous for saying: "It depends." Cases are made up of different facts, and juries respond to them differently. For any sufficiently large set of past outcomes, you start to see reasons why matters should not be treated as like-for-like.

A similar dynamic exists in transactional work when trying to estimate hours, and therefore budget. There is always some idiosyncrasy about a deal that makes a prediction about cost not particularly reliable in any given instance. These things are not wholly random. A seasoned professional can estimate a range with some success, but this is not a prediction in any meaningful sense. Saying it will snow next Christmas is a prediction; saying it will be cold is not, unless you live in the Southern Hemisphere.

Insights abound

Despite these constraints, one can still get useful insights from data, even if those insights are not – in the strictest sense – predictive. You can compare one matter to another and ask what was different about them. Those differences can provide a structured basis for hypothesis testing across matters.

Say, for example, you are trying to guess the number of hours for a real estate deal. You have data on two matters, but the hours, and therefore the cost, diverge widely. You ask the partner who worked on the deal what the difference between them is. The partner explains one real estate transaction is a ground lease (long-term; the tenant usually builds their own structure). The other is a build-to-suit lease (landlord builds a custom facility for the tenant to lease). You go back and get data on more matters to see if the pattern holds. It could be possible the type of property makes a difference, or perhaps there is a list of other factors. The point is that the data give you a way forward in your analysis. You might not find an explanation, but you can at least test theories to see if they are right or wrong. This is the core of what descriptive, diagnostic, and prescriptive analytics can accomplish.

Using these other types of analytics, you can set a range of outcomes that help inform your decision. You might be able to tell your client about all the times you litigated a certain type of matter in the past, what the range of costs was, and frequency distribution of individual matters within that range. The client can then complete a more informed cost–benefit analysis of the possibility of pursuing it further. However, you must be careful to not extend this too far.

Strategy versus operations

Using data to make a best guess on a business decision is not the same as using them to inform strategy once you are in a litigation matter. In this context, litigation strategy means choosing one course of action over another, rather than the above example, which is more of a business decision. Examples of such decisions include whether to file a specific motion, which theory of the case to use, or whether to present a piece of evidence to the jury. These are much more akin to using data in a predictive way, and it suffers for the same reason. If you said that a given type of motion succeeds a certain percentage of the time in a particular type of case, that may be true in a technical sense, but not especially helpful, as it does not take the facts of the case or the weight of the evidence into consideration.

While these limitations constrain strategic prediction, data remain highly effective in operational contexts. For example, consider budgeting: most law firms bill their clients monthly, and many clients put their law firms on budgets. You can work a lot of hours during a month, and – if you do not know where you stand relative to the budget – you can easily exceed it. Going even further, you might want to set budgets that have some empirical basis in past matters. This is where data scientists add measurable value.

Do the various use cases we have covered require a data scientist? Not in all instances. Some are more data engineering challenges; others are straightforward business intelligence or analytics problems. Still, data scientists are the most versatile in this area. They are computational thinkers who can help break down a process for solving a business problem with data. They can apply the quantitative methodology most appropriate to the facts in creative ways. This means you can get more insights than you otherwise would while not using techniques and tools in the wrong way.

Foundations and governance

As organizations begin to operate with data across the enterprise, governance becomes just as critical as the analysis itself. The first reason is to ensure that people can only access the data they should. The second is to ensure you can trust the data themselves.

Governance in access

It is obvious that law firms and legal departments would want to restrict access to internal information by external parties. In the case of the law firm, that includes both its own information and that of its clients. Such information is to be shared only when strictly necessary.

What is less appreciated is the need for internal restrictions. Even partners will only have access to the information they need to do their jobs. They cannot peruse the file of a case they are not working on, nor can they see billing information for their peers.

This is not a problem unique to the legal industry. Access controls exist across all industries and organizations. The issue for law firms and legal departments is that, by virtue of bringing the data together in one place, you have to rethink and reemphasize these controls. Law firms are collecting more data, de-siloing them from unconnected systems, and asking people to use them for analytical purposes. New solutions bring new issues, hence the increased emphasis on this aspect of data security.

Governance in accuracy

Another emerging issue is accuracy of data. The problem is not that information is or was wrong; however, when that information is put to a new use in a new framework, mistakes can happen. Perhaps context on what the data mean is lacking, or they should be cross-referenced with something else when used for a specific purpose. The point is you want the consumers of the information to be able to rely on the numbers they are seeing.

To do this, the data are refined from their raw form into something that end-users can reliably and safely use. Raw data are ingested and preserved in case they are needed again. Those data are cleaned, standardized, de-duplicated, checked for accuracy, and otherwise prepared for downstream use; they are then enriched, aggregated, and parsed to be ready for use. The result is that you have a consistent and agreed-upon dataset, or a "single source of truth". People might still debate the significance of that number or what to do in response, but they can at least operate from a mutually shared set of facts.

Much of the hands-on work to do with infrastructure in governance falls to data engineers. Data stewards or governance teams will define policies, standards, and ownership. However, data scientists still have a role to play:

as end users, they help define the features, schemas, and business logic that are part of the process. That is why governance is generally thought of as part of every data professional's job, rather than a centralized function.

Value

Up to this point, we have only discussed data science in the context of delivery. The remaining question is why it matters. In some instances, the value of what was presented is self-evident – to a practitioner in the field, at least. That is not always the case, and data scientists working in law will be asked at some point why a particular effort or analysis is worth the investment.

Dashboards are only as valuable as the insights they give you. Unless they cause you to look at the world a different way or, better yet, change how you do things, all you have is numbers for the sake of numbers. This is normally not an issue. If a firm goes from doing nothing with its data to having a fully enabled, integrated data and analytics platform, it will learn something and operationalize that lesson to improve the business. But what are those important insights?

Law firms are not normally thought of as capital-intensive businesses. If one takes a wider view and thinks of the attorneys as "human capital", the picture changes. Indeed, most analytics in the legal space are geared toward ensuring that human capital is being deployed in the most economically effective manner. This is not only a question of internal profitability, but – increasingly – one of demonstrable value for clients.

Whether people are being used to their highest and best potential is an inherently difficult question to answer, because all matters are different to a certain extent, and quality of services can be hard to judge. Data are really the only way, and you need to invest in the infrastructure that makes the right data easy to have to hand. Otherwise, it is nearly impossible to establish expectations and monitor performance against those expectations. Perhaps matters should be staffed with cheaper labor (a paralegal instead of a junior associate); maybe there should be budgets for certain phases of deals or even a fixed fee for the whole thing. The only way to answer this question is to see what has been done in the past, and that means data on a sufficiently large sample size of matters.

In theory, the law firm and its client look at the bills that have been sent out over the years to answer these questions. In practice, it requires infrastructure (and the investment that entails) well beyond that which is required to send out invoices and collect on them. There needs to be a way of pressing a button and getting all timesheets on those matters, including billing narratives, task codes, names, rates, hours, and the like. Without that, this type of analysis will have a hard time getting off the ground, because it will just be too difficult.

The specific benefit will depend on what the analysis finds. If it finds a significant amount of time is being spent on work that shouldn't really be performed by outside counsel, the analysis can lead to better scoping. If it turns out more junior employees could be utilized, this finding will then influence staffing. Should the analysis find a common factor as to why some matters get delayed, this could reduce cycle time. In the event that the data are easy to pull and monitor, you have found a way of improving client reporting. The point is that, when someone asks, "Why does this matter?", you have an answer.

Conclusion

Are data scientists the past, present, or future of innovation in the legal industry? The answer is they are a bit of each. Just as they combine skills from different areas, so too will they span different eras of the digital transformation process. The beginnings and endings of these phases will not be clear cut – they never are – but we have come a long way when viewed from the distance of many years.

Data science does not replace professional judgment in legal practice; it structures, tests, and extends it. Its greatest value lies not in predicting outcomes with certainty, but in bringing rigor, consistency, and scale to how decisions are made.

As organizations continue to organize their data and invest in the infrastructure to use it effectively, the supply of insight will continue to grow, alongside demand. Generative AI will accelerate that trend, disrupting established workflows and creating new opportunities for those equipped to harness it.

To return to the earlier metaphor, these developments are part of the same cycle of growth. Data science provides the foundation; legal intelligence is the harvest. Those who cultivate both will be best positioned to navigate what comes next.

Reference

1 American Bar Association, "Uniform Task-Based Management System (UTBMS)", 2026. See: https://www.americanbar.org/groups/litigation/resources/uniform-task-based-management-system/.

Chapter 4:
Knowledge management, prompt engineering, and the quiet infrastructure of legal AI

By Colin S. Levy, general counsel, Malbek

Where the real value lives

In November 2023, Allen & Overy (now A&O Shearman) became the first major law firm to deploy a generative artificial intelligence (AI) tool across its entire global practice. Harvey, built on OpenAI's GPT-4, went live for 3,500 lawyers in 43 offices. Within the trial period, they submitted roughly 40,000 queries to the system.[1] By any measure, the rollout was fast. However, the more interesting number was one that attracted less attention: the firm's knowledge management (KM) team had spent months beforehand preparing the ground, structuring the firm's internal knowledge so the tool could draw on it reliably, and building prompt templates calibrated to the firm's own standards.

That preparation made the difference between a capable tool and a useful one. Other firms have since learned the same lesson – sometimes, the hard way. Clifford Chance, Linklaters, and a growing number of mid-size and boutique firms have all deployed generative AI in some form. The technology is now widely available. However, the gap between having access to a tool and getting dependable value from it remains large, and that gap turns out to be a KM problem, rather than a technology problem.

This chapter examines three forces that are converging to reshape how legal knowledge is produced, managed, and delivered to clients. It looks at what day-to-day AI use actually means for practicing lawyers; how prompt engineering – the practice of structuring the instructions given to a generative AI system to produce reliable, task-appropriate output – is settling into legal work as a baseline skill, rather than a specialty; and how KM teams are emerging as the critical link between raw AI capability and reliable work product. Prompt engineering matters, but it matters in service of a larger knowledge system; this framing underlines the rest of the chapter.

What generative AI use looks like in legal practice

Dispelling the demo myth

Anyone who has attended a legal technology conference recently has seen the demonstration: a vendor types a short instruction into a chatbot, and a polished motion appears on screen within seconds. The implication is that this is effortless. In practice, the output from a single prompt is rarely usable as delivered. It requires iteration, checking, restructuring, and the application of professional judgment at every stage. Lawyers who use these tools daily report that the value lies not in the initial response, but in a broader workflow of prompting, verifying, and refining.

The "magic prompt" narrative, which suggests that generative AI eliminates the need for legal expertise, has done real damage by setting expectations that lead to disillusionment. Firms that have moved past that phase tend to describe AI as an amplifier of professional judgment, rather than a substitute for it. The more skill a lawyer brings to the interaction, the better the output.

This framing has practical consequences. If AI is an amplifier, the question is then not whether to use it, but how to use it well. That shifts attention from the technology to the human skills involved in its implementation: the quality of the prompts; the rigor of the verification; and the depth of the knowledge base the tool draws on. These are areas where legal professionals and KM teams have real expertise, which helps explain why the best outcomes tend to come from firms that treat AI adoption as a professional development challenge, rather than a technology procurement exercise.

How lawyers are using it

A 2024 survey by the American Bar Association (ABA) found that 30 percent of lawyers now use AI tools, up from 11 percent the prior year.[2] The Clio Legal Trends Report for the same period documented an even steeper rise, with self-reported adoption among legal professionals jumping from 19 percent to 79 percent.[3] Those numbers sit in apparent tension with an Embroker survey from the same year, which found that 78 percent of US law firms were not using any AI tools at all.[4] The discrepancy reflects differences in methodology, rather than contradictory realities: surveys asking individual lawyers about any use, including informal experimentation, produce higher numbers than surveys asking firms about sanctioned, firm-wide deployment. The direction is consistent across all of them. Adoption is growing, and it is clustering around specific, repeatable tasks.

The most common application is first draft generation for routine documents. Engagement letters, standard memos, and client update emails are typical candidates. The ABA survey found that 77 percent of AI-using lawyers employ the technology for document drafting.[5] Nobody treats the output as a final product, but a workable first draft that saves 30–60 minutes of initial writing time is valuable when multiplied across dozens of matters.

Research synthesis is the second major use case. Lawyers use AI to digest lengthy regulatory guidance, pull key facts from deposition transcripts, or summarize case law on narrow issues. Thomson Reuters CoCounsel, for instance, has built structured summarization and timeline generation into its core offering.[6] Firms that have integrated AI with their document management systems (iManage, NetDocuments, and similar platforms) are also using it for internal knowledge retrieval, enabling associates to query the firm's own precedent bank in natural language, rather than relying on keyword searches.

Beyond these workhorses, lawyers report using AI to reformat work product for different audiences – converting a dense analysis into a client-friendly summary, for example – and as a brainstorming tool for issue-spotting, presenting a set of facts and asking the model to surface risks or alternative framings they may not have considered. This last use case is particularly interesting, because it treats the AI not as a drafter, but as a sounding board. Partners who use the tool this way describe it as similar to talking through a problem with a knowledgeable colleague who happens to have read everything you have ever written and everything in the firm's precedent bank.

The time savings are real. Everlaw's 2025 survey found that lawyers using generative AI save roughly 240 hours per year, or about 32 working days.[7] Clio's data suggest that 65 percent of AI-using lawyers save between one and five hours per week.[8] At Linklaters, the firm's internal chatbot Laila, built on Microsoft Azure OpenAI, now handles upwards of 60,000 prompts per week.[9] Clifford Chance reported that, by April 2024, more than 60 percent of its global workforce was using Microsoft 365 Copilot daily.[10]

What lawyers are not using it for

Equally telling is where lawyers draw the line. Very few firms permit AI-generated content to reach a client or a court without human review. Novel legal analysis in high-stakes matters remains the province of experienced practitioners. Anything involving current, jurisdiction-specific procedural rules is treated with caution, because the training data behind most large language models (LLMs) do not reliably reflect recent changes.

The honest acknowledgment of these limits is itself a form of competence. Firms that are candid about what AI can and cannot do reliably tend to use it more effectively than those that either oversell the technology or refuse to engage with it. The ABA's 2024 survey bears this out: the lawyers who report the highest satisfaction with AI tools are also the ones who describe the most structured, bounded use cases.[11] They are using AI for what it is good at, and routing everything else to human judgment.

The Thomson Reuters 2025 generative AI survey found that concerns about AI hallucinations – the tendency of LLMs to fabricate plausible-sounding but false information – remain the most widely cited barrier to deeper adoption across the legal profession.[12] As the examples later in this chapter will show, that caution is well-founded.

Prompt engineering as a legal skill

From casual query to professional instruction

Prompt engineering, as noted above, is the practice of structuring the instructions given to a generative AI system to produce reliable, task-appropriate output. In legal work, it amounts to embedding professional judgment – jurisdictional context, subject-matter constraints, audience calibration, and format specifications – into the instruction itself. The reason it matters is practical, rather than technical. Legal work demands a precision that a casually worded prompt will not produce. "Summarize this contract" will generate a summary, but it will probably miss the provisions that matter to the specific client, ignore the governing law, and pitch the language at the wrong level for its intended reader.

Consider two approaches to the same task:

> **Prompt A:** "Review this agreement and tell me about any risks."
> **Prompt B:** "You are acting as outside counsel advising a US-based software company that is the buyer in this asset purchase agreement governed by Delaware law. Identify any indemnification provisions that deviate from a standard mutual indemnification position, flag the specific language, and suggest redline alternatives. Present your findings in a table with columns for clause number, current language, risk assessment, and proposed revision. Do not include provisions that conform to market standard."

Prompt B produces dramatically better output – not because the AI is smarter, but because the lawyer has embedded professional judgment in the instruction itself. The North Carolina Bar Association's 2024 guidance on prompt engineering for lawyers frames the shift as one from asking questions to issuing instructions, emphasizing granular specificity over general queries.[13] Lawyers who attain consistently good results tend to frame the model's role explicitly, specify what to look for and what to ignore, set jurisdictional and topical constraints, and tell the model what format to use for its output. They also work iteratively, treating the first response as a starting point and refining through follow-up prompts, rather than expecting a single query to produce a finished product.

This iterative pattern mirrors the way lawyers have always worked with junior colleagues. You give an instruction, review the result, provide feedback, and sharpen the analysis through successive rounds. The difference is speed: what used to take days of back-and-forth can now happen in minutes.

A 2025 randomized controlled trial published in the *Harvard Journal of Law and Technology Digest* found that legal AI tools built on retrieval-augmented generation (RAG) architecture produced statistically significant improvements in clarity, organization, and professionalism across multiple task types.[14] Those improvements depended heavily on how the tool was used. Lawyers who provided structured, specific prompts achieved materially better results than those who asked open-ended questions. The study reinforces what practitioners have been discovering informally: the quality of the prompt is at least as important as the quality of the model.

Box 1: Anatomy of an effective legal prompt

An effective legal prompt typically contains five layers, each encoding a different dimension of professional judgment:

1. *Role and context:* "You are acting as a senior corporate associate in a US law firm advising the buyer in a cross-border acquisition." This shapes the model's assumptions about the level of sophistication expected.
2. *Specific task:* "Identify all representations and warranties that fall below market standard for a transaction of this size." Precision eliminates the ambiguity that leads to generic output.
3. *Constraints:* "Apply Delaware law. Do not address tax representations, as these are being reviewed separately." Constraints reduce the risk of hallucinated analysis outside the prompt's intended scope.

4. *Output format:* "Present findings in a table with columns for clause number, current language, market standard comparison, risk rating, and suggested revision." Format specification ensures the output is immediately usable.
5. *Iteration plan:* "After your initial review, I will ask you to draft a client-ready summary of the three highest-risk items." Building in a second step signals that the first output is a working draft.

The failure modes

Poor prompting in legal work has consequences. The most common error is overreliance on a single prompt, treating the model's initial output as a final product without iteration. Close behind is hallucination amplification: vague, open-ended prompts invite the model to fill gaps with fabricated information. A prompt like "Find me cases that support the argument that..." without specifying a jurisdiction, court level, or date range is an invitation for fabricated citations that look authentic.

Context window mismanagement is a subtler problem. Uploading hundreds of pages of contracts, correspondence, and due diligence materials into a single prompt can overwhelm the model's ability to maintain focus, producing output that misses critical details or ignores instructions buried in the mass of input. And audience mismatch – output pitched too technically for a board or too simply for co-counsel – wastes the time the tool was meant to save.

These failure modes are not merely theoretical. They show up in the court sanctions discussed later in this chapter, and they are the reason unstructured, ad-hoc prompting by individual lawyers is giving way to governed, firm-wide prompt libraries maintained by KM teams. That shift, from individual experimentation to institutional capability, is in many respects the central story of legal AI adoption so far, and it is a story about KM as much as about prompts.

The KM team as adoption engine

The evolving role of legal KM

For decades, KM in law firms meant maintaining precedent databases, curating know-how collections, and managing template libraries. Those functions still matter, but they have been joined by something much larger. KM teams are now expected to make AI tools usable, reliable, and trusted across the firm. In practical terms, this means structuring knowledge so AI tools can retrieve it accurately; building and governing prompt libraries; designing practice-specific training; and running the feedback systems that keep everything improving. KM has always been about connecting people with the right knowledge at the right time. Generative AI is a powerful new channel for that mission, but the channel only works if the knowledge flowing through it is accurate, current, and properly structured.

Many firms have learned this the hard way. Deploying a generative AI tool without investing in the knowledge infrastructure that supports it tends to produce disappointing results, no matter how capable the underlying model.

Prompt libraries as a KM asset

One of the more consequential developments in legal AI has been the emergence of firm-level prompt libraries: curated collections of reusable prompt templates, organized by practice area and task type. These differ from document templates in an important way. A document template captures the structure and language of a finished product, but a prompt template captures the reasoning process: the questions to ask, the order in which to ask them; the constraints that prevent common errors; and the output format best suited to a particular audience. Where a document template says, "Here is how to write it," a prompt template says, "Here is how to think about it."

Firms are building these for contract review calibrated to specific agreement types; for due diligence issue-spotting organized by deal category; and for client alert drafting that embeds the firm's house style. Legal technology platforms are supporting the trend. LEAP US provides AI prompt templates that auto-populate with matter-specific information. Harvey AI, now deployed across roughly half of the AmLaw 100 firms, offers workflow templates that firms can tailor to their own standards.[15]

The governance question that follows is important: who owns the prompt library, who maintains it, and who quality-controls templates before they go firm-wide? In most firms that have addressed this, the answer points to the KM team. This makes sense: KM professionals already manage template libraries, precedent banks, and know-how databases. Prompt libraries are a natural extension of that work, although they require different skills. Evaluating whether a prompt produces reliable output across different document types and models is closer to quality assurance than to traditional legal knowledge curation, and some firms are hiring accordingly.

What effective KM-led AI adoption looks like

The most successful AI adoption programs share a common feature: KM is deeply involved at every stage.

Curating and validating prompt libraries, discussed above, is a natural KM function. An associate may develop a useful prompt for reviewing software licensing agreements but, before it becomes part of the firm's standard toolkit, someone needs to test it against known benchmarks, refine the language, and check that it produces consistent results across different models and document types. That someone is typically the KM team.

Building AI-ready knowledge bases is harder and less glamorous. The effectiveness of RAG systems, the architecture underlying most firm-deployed legal AI tools, depends entirely on the quality of the knowledge base they draw from. A precedent bank filled with outdated templates, inconsistently formatted clauses, and poorly tagged documents produces mediocre AI output, regardless of the model's sophistication. Making a corpus AI-ready requires systematic review: identifying which documents belong in the RAG knowledge base; standardizing metadata; removing superseded versions; and tagging materials by practice area, jurisdiction, and date. A typical mid-size firm's precedent bank contains tens of thousands of documents accumulated over decades. The cleanup is painstaking, but it is the foundation on which every other AI capability rests.

Training is the third piece. An Embroker survey in 2024 found that the majority of firms provide no formal AI training at all.[16] The KM teams that have stepped into this gap report better results when training is embedded in practice groups and tailored to specific workflows. Showing a corporate associate how to use AI to review a share purchase agreement is more effective than a firm-wide webinar on what AI can do in the abstract. The most effective programs appear to share a few traits: they use live matters as the teaching material, with appropriate safeguards; they pair associates with experienced lawyers who can verify output in context; they include explicit instruction on failure modes and verification techniques; and they treat AI fluency as a competency developed progressively over many months, rather than in a one-time session. Firms that have adopted this approach report faster progression from pilot to routine use, and noticeably fewer of the kinds of errors that end up in sanctions orders.

Finally, effective programs establish feedback loops. Lawyers report what works and what fails, and that information feeds back into prompt refinement, tool configuration, and knowledge base curation. Without this loop, the firm's AI capability flatlines after the initial rollout.

The organizational design that supports all of this varies. Some firms have created dedicated AI roles within KM – titles like "director of legal AI" or "AI knowledge engineer" are appearing in job postings. Others have embedded AI specialists within practice groups, reporting to both the practice leader and the head of KM. What matters less than the structure is the principle: someone with KM expertise needs to own the interface between the technology and the people who use it. Where that role is absent or diffuse, adoption tends to be uneven and unsustainable.

Scaling down: KM principles at mid-size and smaller firms

Most of the well-documented examples of KM-led AI adoption come from global firms with dedicated KM departments and substantial budgets. The principles, however, scale down. A mid-size firm may not employ a director of legal AI, but it can designate a KM-aware partner or counsel to own prompt governance across practice groups. A boutique firm may not maintain a thousand-document precedent bank, but the hundred templates it does maintain can be cleaned, tagged, and made AI-ready by a single focused effort. Solo and small-firm practitioners, working without institutional KM support, are experimenting with shared prompt libraries assembled through bar association sections and practice-area communities, and some jurisdiction-specific vendors are beginning to offer managed prompt libraries as a subscription service. The scale differs; the underlying discipline – curating knowledge, governing prompts, training users, gathering feedback – does not.

Organizational challenges

None of this is easy. Resistance from partners who see AI as a threat to the billable hour model remains common, particularly at firms where revenue is closely tied to time-based billing. If AI reduces the hours required for a task, the revenue implications are real, and partners are not wrong to notice. The productive response is to engage with the pricing question, rather than avoid the technology: fixed fees, value-based pricing, and hybrid models all become more viable when AI reduces the cost of delivery. However, that conversation has been slow to develop at many firms, and KM teams often find themselves pushing for adoption into a headwind of economic anxiety that the technology itself has created.

The "shadow AI" problem may be more urgent. A survey of 300 corporate legal departments found that 81 percent were using unapproved AI tools without proper data controls.[17] Lawyers who cannot access approved tools through their firm, or who find them cumbersome, simply use consumer-grade alternatives on personal devices. The risk is not theoretical: a single upload of privileged documents to an unauthorized platform can waive attorney–client privilege. Most KM leaders who have addressed this argue that the solution is not a ban, but better-designed approved tools that lawyers actually want to use.

Resource constraints compound everything. KM teams are being asked to lead AI transformation without additional headcount or budget. Firms that treat KM as overhead, rather than infrastructure, tend to underinvest in exactly the capabilities that determine whether their AI tools deliver value.

There is also a credibility dimension. KM professionals who are not practicing lawyers sometimes face skepticism from partners who view AI guidance from non-lawyers as insufficiently grounded in the realities of practice. The most effective KM teams address this by working closely with "champion" associates and counsel within each practice group: lawyers who pilot tools, develop prompts in the context of live matters, and lend professional credibility to the rollout. This champion network model, in which KM provides the infrastructure and practice group allies provide the context, appears repeatedly in the firms that have moved past the pilot stage.

Practical examples: Successes and failures

A&O Shearman and Harvey: Prompt-driven contract review

A&O Shearman's deployment of Harvey AI remains the most publicly documented example of large-scale legal AI adoption. During the trial period beginning in late 2023, the firm's 3,500 lawyers generated approximately 40,000 queries, applying the tool to live client work across practice areas.[18] The firm has since expanded the deployment and begun building agentic AI systems for more complex workflows.

What made the rollout work, according to the firm's own public statements, was the infrastructure around the tool. The KM team developed prompt templates calibrated to specific practice areas and document types. Contract review prompts were structured around the firm's own clause libraries and internal standards, so the AI's output reflected A&O Shearman's approach, rather than generic analysis. The firm reports that attorneys save an estimated seven hours on average per contract review when using the tool.

The governance model is worth noting. A&O Shearman established a central AI steering committee that includes partners from major practice groups, alongside KM and technology leadership. New prompt templates and AI workflows go through a review process before firm-wide deployment, similar to the approval process for precedent documents. Prompts are versioned, tagged by author and date, and retired when they become outdated. This governance layer is part of what distinguishes a sustainable, firm-wide capability from a loose collection of individual experiments.

A&O Shearman also built ContractMatrix, which the firm describes as the first AI application designed specifically for in-house counsel, developed in collaboration with Harvey and Microsoft.[19] The tool allows the firm's clients to manage and analyze their own contracts using AI grounded in A&O Shearman's legal expertise. This represents the trajectory that many firms are trying to follow: moving from internal efficiency tools to client-facing products built on the same KM infrastructure.

Clifford Chance and Linklaters: Competing approaches to firm-wide adoption

Clifford Chance took a different path. The firm partnered with Microsoft to deploy 365 Copilot across its global workforce and reported that, by April 2024, more than 60 percent of staff were using it daily.[20] Rather than building a bespoke legal AI tool, Clifford Chance integrated generative AI into the applications lawyers already used (Word, Outlook, Teams), reducing the friction of adoption. The firm also developed a proprietary tool called Clifford Chance Assist for tasks requiring more specialized legal reasoning.

Linklaters, meanwhile, built its own internal chatbot, Laila, on Azure OpenAI. The tool now handles upwards of 60,000 prompts per week. Linklaters also ran an "AI Sandbox" program that invited employees across the firm to propose AI use cases, generating 75 proposals that fed into the firm's AI strategy.[21] This bottom-up approach, combining centralized infrastructure with decentralized experimentation, represents an increasingly common model for adoption.

What these three firms have in common is instructive. All three invested heavily in KM infrastructure before or alongside the technology deployment. All three embedded AI into existing workflows, rather than asking lawyers to adopt a new, standalone tool, and created mechanisms for lawyers to feed their experiences back into the system, so the tools got better over time. The technology platforms they chose differ, but the organizational approach is strikingly similar.

Mata v. Avianca and its aftermath: The cost of skipping guardrails

The most widely cited cautionary tale in legal AI remains *Mata v. Avianca*, decided in the US District Court for the Southern District of New York in June 2023. Two attorneys submitted a motion supported by six case citations, all generated by ChatGPT, none of which existed.[22] The fabricated cases included fictitious party names, invented quotations, and fabricated internal citations. When opposing counsel challenged the references, the attorneys responded by asking ChatGPT to confirm they were real and submitted that confirmation to the court. The judge imposed a $5,000 fine.

The root cause was not the technology. The prompt was vague and open-ended; there was no verification step; and the firm had no protocol for AI-assisted research. Every layer of protection that should have existed was absent. The case has since been cited in virtually every judicial discussion of AI in legal practice, and it accelerated a wave of judicial response. Judge Brantley Starr of the Northern District of Texas issued one of the first standing orders requiring lawyers to certify either that no AI was used to draft a filing or that any AI-generated content was verified by a human.[23] Similar standing orders have since been issued by judges in the Eastern District of Pennsylvania, the Northern District of Illinois, and the Court of International Trade, among others, and several state supreme courts have issued general guidance on AI use in filings.[24,25,26,27]

Subsequent incidents have reinforced the pattern. In July 2025, two attorneys representing MyPillow CEO Mike Lindell were each fined $3,000 in US District Court in Colorado after a filing was discovered to contain more than 24 fabricated case citations.[28] In April 2026, an attorney in Oregon federal court was sanctioned approximately $109,700 after submitting filings that cited 15 nonexistent cases and included eight fabricated quotations attributed to real legal authorities.[29] In each case, the problem was not AI use per se, but AI use without the institutional guardrails – prompt discipline, verification protocols, KM oversight – that would have caught the errors before they reached the court.

The adoption plateau: A pattern, not an anecdote

A different kind of failure is harder to see because it does not produce headlines. Industry data suggest that the majority of legal AI deployments stall after an initial burst of enthusiasm. Even among firms that do adopt, usage frequently plateaus. Analysis by Axiom has found that the vast majority of legal AI pilot programs fail to deliver measurable business impact.[30]

The diagnosis is consistent across these cases: training was generic rather than practice-specific; the tool was not integrated into existing workflows; prompts bore little resemblance to the work lawyers actually do; and there was no mechanism to capture feedback and improve the system over time. These are KM problems, not technology problems. The firms that address them – A&O Shearman, Clifford Chance, and Linklaters among them – see sustained adoption. Those that do not see expensive pilots that quietly wind down.

The pattern has a notable implication for how firms budget for AI. The license fee for the technology is typically the smallest part of the investment. The larger costs are in the KM infrastructure: cleaning up knowledge bases, building prompt libraries, training lawyers in practice-specific workflows, and staffing the feedback loop that keeps the system improving. Firms that budget only for the technology and assume adoption will take care of itself are, based on the available evidence, setting themselves up for the plateau.

The client-facing future

From internal efficiency to external value

Most firms started using generative AI to do existing work faster. The early movers are now pushing into a second phase: using AI to deliver value to clients in new ways. A&O Shearman's ContractMatrix is one example. Regulatory monitoring dashboards, tailored to specific clients and maintained by KM teams, are another. The competitive question is shifting from "Do we have AI tools?" to "Does our AI-powered knowledge infrastructure benefit our clients?"

Client expectations are moving accordingly. In-house counsel increasingly ask prospective firms about their AI capabilities, using them as a proxy for efficiency and innovation. Several major corporate legal departments now include AI capability questions in their requests for proposal. A Thomson Reuters survey found that 78 percent of lawyers expect generative AI to become central to their workflow within five years.[31] Firms that can point to concrete, client-relevant applications showing the work, rather than simply asserting innovation, will have a meaningful advantage in pitches and panel reviews.

The pricing conversation

The financial dimension is worth stating plainly. If AI saves approximately 240 hours per lawyer per year, a figure consistent with multiple surveys, firms face a decision about where that value goes.[32] Some will flow to clients through lower costs and faster turnaround. Some will flow to the firm through higher-value work made possible by the time freed up. The firms that manage this reallocation thoughtfully, with input from KM teams who understand both the tools and the workflows, will be better positioned than those that let it happen by default.

The alternative to the hourly model is not a single alternative but a family of them, and AI makes several of them more workable. Fixed-fee arrangements become more attractive when the firm can estimate delivery cost with greater confidence, because AI reduces the variance in how long routine tasks take. Subscription or retainer models, in which a client pays for ongoing access to a defined scope of advisory work, become more viable when the firm can deliver that work more efficiently. Outcome- or success-based fees, long discussed and rarely adopted, become more credible when AI-enabled throughput allows the firm to absorb the risk. Phased pricing, in which different stages of a matter carry different fee structures – fixed for triage, hourly for bespoke advisory, contingent for final adjudication – maps well onto workflows where AI handles the repeatable pieces and human judgment handles the rest. None of these is a universal answer, but each responds to a pressure that AI has intensified, rather than created, and the firms that develop a considered answer will be better positioned than those that hold the hourly model in place by default.

What client-facing AI looks like in practice

Several models are emerging. Regulatory monitoring dashboards, maintained by KM teams and tailored to specific industries, track legislative and regulatory changes and alert clients in something close to real time. Self-service portals for routine questions – employment law FAQs, compliance checklists, contract playbooks – give clients immediate answers while flagging complex issues for human follow-up. These tools do not replace legal advice; they extend the firm's reach into the gaps between formal instructions.

A third model involves AI-assisted matter updates: status summaries generated from the matter file and reviewed by the responsible lawyer before delivery, giving clients visibility without requiring a call. The most ambitious approaches involve genuine co-creation, with in-house teams and outside counsel working within the same AI-powered environment. A&O Shearman's ContractMatrix points in this direction, giving in-house counsel direct access to AI tools grounded in the firm's legal expertise.

Each of these models requires sustained KM involvement. A regulatory dashboard is only as good as the curated content it draws on. A self-service portal loses credibility if its knowledge base is not kept current. A client-facing tool that is deployed and then neglected is worse than no tool at all, because it actively erodes the trust it was designed to build. The common thread is that client-facing AI is not a product you launch. It is a service you maintain, and that maintenance is a KM function.

Box 2: Five questions to ask before deploying a client-facing AI tool

1. *What happens when it is wrong?* Every AI system will occasionally produce inaccurate output. Before a tool reaches clients, define the error-handling protocol: who reviews, how quickly errors are corrected, and how the client is notified.
2. *Which data flow through the system?* Client-facing AI must meet the same confidentiality standards as any channel for privileged information. Data governance must cover storage, processing location, and access controls.
3. *Does it solve a real problem?* If the primary motivation is to appear innovative, the tool is unlikely to sustain client engagement. It should reduce response times, improve knowledge access, or enable self-service for genuinely routine questions.
4. *How will success be measured?* Useful metrics include client usage rates, satisfaction scores, reduction in routine inquiries, and whether the tool generates new bespoke advisory instructions.
5. *Who maintains it?* A client-facing tool that is not regularly updated with current analysis and refined prompts will lose credibility fast. Ongoing KM curation is a prerequisite, not an afterthought.

The trust and ethics dimension

Client-facing AI raises the stakes on accuracy, confidentiality, and professional responsibility. Every output that reaches a client carries the firm's reputation. KM teams are central to establishing the guardrails: defining what gets automated, what requires human review, and where the firm draws the line.

The regulatory landscape is filling in. The California State Bar's 2023 practical guidance on generative AI emphasizes that the duty of competence extends to AI tools and that confidentiality obligations do not evaporate at the prompt window.[33] The Florida Bar's Ethics Opinion 24-1, issued in 2024, reaches similar conclusions and adds specific guidance on client disclosure and billing for AI-assisted work.[34] The New York State Bar Association's 2024 report on AI takes a broader view, addressing unauthorized practice of law concerns and the duty of supervision over AI-generated work product.[35] The ABA's Formal Opinion 512 has become a common reference point across jurisdictions.[36] The details vary, but the common thread is consistent: lawyers remain responsible for their work product, and the tools used to produce it do not diminish that responsibility.

Transparency about AI use is becoming both an ethical obligation and a source of competitive advantage. Clients who understand how a firm uses AI, and what safeguards are in place, are more likely to trust the output. Firms that proactively explain their AI governance, publish review protocols, and invite questions about how technology contributes to work product are building a form of credibility that less open competitors will struggle to match.

The professional responsibility dimension deserves specific attention. What is already clear is that the duty of competence extends to the tools a lawyer uses. A lawyer who submits AI-generated analysis without understanding how it was produced, or without verifying its accuracy, is not meeting that duty. KM teams can help by building verification into the workflow itself, making it a structural feature of the tool, rather than something that depends on individual discipline.

Conclusion

The story of AI in legal practice so far has a consistent theme. The technology works, but only when it is supported by the right institutional infrastructure. A&O Shearman's Harvey deployment works because of prompt libraries and structured knowledge bases. Clifford Chance's Copilot adoption works because the tool was embedded in existing workflows. *Mata v. Avianca* happened because none of those safeguards were in place.

For KM professionals, this is a moment of unusual leverage. The function that has often been viewed as a support role now sits at the center of the most consequential operational change in legal practice in years. The firms that get this right will be the ones where KM teams are properly resourced, closely connected to practice groups, and treated as infrastructure, rather than overhead. For practicing lawyers, the implication is more measured than the early hype suggested. Prompt engineering is a skill worth investing in, but it is one skill among many, and it is most valuable when supported by the knowledge infrastructure around it. How well a lawyer communicates with AI tools will shape the quality of their work product in the same way that research and drafting skills always have, but the tools themselves will only ever be as reliable as the knowledge system they draw on.

The competitive question for the next several years is already taking shape. It will not be decided by which firm licenses the best AI model. The 2025 benchmark study published by LawSites found that the leading legal AI platforms now offer broadly comparable capabilities, and that the differences between tools are smaller than the differences between how well-prepared firms deploy them.[37] The differentiator will be the knowledge systems, prompt discipline, and client-facing vision that make those models reliably useful in the context of a specific firm's practice. A&O Shearman, Clifford Chance, and Linklaters have each made substantial investments in that infrastructure. The evidence from their experiences suggests that the work is unglamorous, the payoff is real, and the firms that delay are accumulating a deficit that will become harder to close as the early movers build on their lead.

References

1 Wakeling D, "A&O announces exclusive launch partnership with Harvey", A&O Shearman, 15 February 2023. See: https://www.aoshearman.com/en/news/ao-announces-exclusive-launch-partnership-with-harvey.

2 Calaguas M, "2024 Artificial Intelligence TechReport", American Bar Association, 25 April 2025. See: https://www.americanbar.org/groups/law_practice/resources/tech-report/2024/2024-artificial-intelligence-techreport/.

3 Clio, *The 2024 Legal Trends Report*, October 2024. See: https://www.clio.com/uk/resources/legal-trends/2024-report/.

4 Embroker, *From 22% to 80%: How AI in Legal Practice Took Off in 2025*, 26 May 2026. See: https://www.embroker.com/blog/ai-in-legal-practice/.

5 Calaguas M, "2024 Artificial Intelligence TechReport", American Bar Association, 25 April 2025. See: https://www.americanbar.org/groups/law_practice/resources/tech-report/2024/2024-artificial-intelligence-techreport/.

6 Thomson Reuters, "CoCounsel: The industry-leading AI for professionals", 2026. See: https://www.thomsonreuters.com/en/cocounsel.

7 Smith J, "Lawyers Report Saving up to 32.5 Working Days per Year with Generative AI", Everlaw, 22 July 2025. See: https://www.everlaw.com/blog/ai-and-law/lawyers-report-saving-up-to-32-5-working-days-per-year-with-generative-ai/.

8 Clio, The 2024 Legal Trends Report, October 2024. See: https://www.clio.com/uk/resources/legal-trends/2024-report/.

9 Linklaters, "Linklaters launches AI Sandbox following second global ideas campaign", 2 December 2024. See: https://www.linklaters.com/about-us/news-and-deals/news/2024/december/linklaters-launches-ai-sandbox-following-second-globa l-ideas-campaign.
10 Greenwood P and Malhotra-Denny S, "Clifford Chance expands use of generative AI with deployment of Copilot for Microsoft 365 and Viva Suite for its global workforce", Clifford Chance, 28 February 2024. See: https://www.cliffordchance.com/news/news/2024/02/clifford-chance-generative-ai-microsoft.html.
11 Calaguas M, "2024 Artificial Intelligence TechReport", American Bar Association, 25 April 2025. See: https://www.americanbar.org/groups/law_practice/resources/tech-report/2024/2024-artificial-intelligence-techreport/.
12 Warren Z, Abbott M, Leach L et al, 2025 *Generative AI in Professional Services Report*, Thomas Reuters Institute, 2025. See: https://www.thomsonreuters.com/en/reports/2025-generative-ai-in-professional-services-report.
13 Reach C, "Prompt Engineering 101 for Lawyers", North Carolina Bar Association, 21 August 2024. See: https://www.ncbar.org/nc-lawyer/2024-08/prompt-engineering-101-for-lawyers/.
14 Johnston P, "Retrieval-augmented generation (RAG): towards a promising LLM architecture for legal work?", *Harvard Journal of Law and Technology Digest*, 2 April 2025. See: https://jolt.law.harvard.edu/digest/retrieval-augmented-generation-rag-towards-a-promising-llm-architecture-for-legal-work.
15 Ambrogi RJ, "Legal AI Tools Show Promise in First-of-its-Kind Benchmark Study, with Harvey and CoCounsel Leading the Pack", LawSites, 28 February 2025. See: https://www.lawnext.com/2025/02/legal-ai-tools-show-promise-in-first-of-its-kind-benchmark-study-with-harvey-and-cocounsel-leading-the-pack.html.
16 Embroker, *From 22% to 80%: How AI in Legal Practice Took Off in 2025*, 26 May 2026. See: https://www.embroker.com/blog/ai-in-legal-practice/.
17 Barnes L, "Your Firm Is The Last One Talking About Whether To Adopt AI", The AI Law, 30 April 2026. See: https://www.theailaw.xyz/p/your-firm-is-the-last-one-talking-about-whether-to-adopt-ai.
18 Wakeling D, "A&O announces exclusive launch partnership with Harvey", A&O Shearman, 15 February 2023. See: https://www.aoshearman.com/en/news/ao-announces-exclusive-launch-partnership-with-harvey.
19 Harvey AI, "A&O Shearman: Transforming Legal Services through AI Innovation", 2026. See: https://www.harvey.ai/customers/a-and-o-shearman.
20 Greenwood P and Malhotra-Denny S, "Clifford Chance expands use of generative AI with deployment of Copilot for Microsoft 365 and Viva Suite for its global workforce", Clifford Chance, 28 February 2024. See: https://www.cliffordchance.com/news/news/2024/02/clifford-chance-generative-ai-microsoft.html.

21 Linklaters, "Linklaters launches AI Sandbox following second global ideas campaign", 2 December 2024. See: https://www.linklaters.com/about-us/news-and-deals/news/2024/december/linklaters-launches-ai-sandbox-following-second-global-ideas-campaign.

22 *Mata v. Avianca, Inc.*, No. 22-cv-1461 (S.D.N.Y. June 22, 2023).

23 Volokh E, "Federal Judge Requires All Lawyers to File Certificates Related to Use of Generative AI", Reason, 30 May 2023. See: https://reason.com/volokh/2023/05/30/federal-judge-requires-all-lawyers-to-file-certificates-related-to-use-of-generative-ai/.

24 Baylson MM, "STANDING ORDER RE: ARTIFICIAL INTELLIGENCE ("AI") IN CASES ASSIGNED TO JUDGE BAYLSON", United States District Court for the Eastern District of Pennsylvania, 6 June 2023. See: https://www.paed.uscourts.gov/sites/paed/files/documents/procedures/Standing%20Order%20Re%20Artificial%20Intelligence%206.6.pdf.

25 Fuentes GA, "Standing Order for Civil Cases Before Magistrate Judge Fuentes", United States District Court for the Northern District of Illinois, 3 March 2026. See: https://www.ilnd.uscourts.gov/_assets/_documents/_forms/_judges/Fuentes/Standing%20order%20for%20civil%20cases%20beofre%20Magistrate%20Judge%20Fuentes%20with%20appendix.pdf.

26 Vaden SA, "ORDER ON ARTIFICIAL INTELLIGENCE", United States Court of International Trade, 8 June 2023. See: https://www.cit.uscourts.gov/sites/cit/files/Order%20on%20Artificial%20Intelligence.pdf.

27 Supreme Court of Illinois, *Illinois Supreme Court Policy on Artificial Intelligence*, 18 December 2024. See: https://ilcourtsaudio.blob.core.windows.net/antilles-resources/resources/e43964ab-8874-4b7a-be4e-63af019cb6f7/Illinois%20Supreme%20Court%20AI%20Policy.pdf.

28 Coomer v. Lindell, 2025 U.S. Dist. LEXIS 128372, No. 1:22-cv-01129-NYW-SBP (D. Colo. July 7, 2025).

29 Couvrette v. Wisnovsky, No. 1:21-cv-00157-CL (D. Or. Mar. 23, 2026).

30 Axiom, "AI for In-House Legal Teams: A Practical Playbook for Fast, Safe Wins", November 2025. See: https://www.axiomlaw.com/blog/ai-for-in-house-legal-teams-playbook.

31 Warren Z, Abbott M, Leach L et al, *2025 Generative AI in Professional Services Report*, Thomas Reuters Institute, 2025. See: https://www.thomsonreuters.com/en/reports/2025-generative-ai-in-professional-services-report.

32 Smith J, "Lawyers Report Saving up to 32.5 Working Days per Year with Generative AI", Everlaw, 22 July 2025. See: https://www.everlaw.com/blog/ai-and-law/lawyers-report-saving-up-to-32-5-working-days-per-year-with-generative-ai/.

33 State Bar of California Standing Committee on Professional Responsibility and Conduct, *Practical Guidance for the Use of Generative Artificial Intelligence in the Practice of Law*, State Bar of California, 16 November 2023. See: https://www.calbar.ca.gov/Portals/0/documents/ethics/Generative-AI-Practical-Guidance.pdf.

34 The Florida Bar, *Ethics Opinion 24-1*, 19 January 2024. See: https://www.floridabar.org/etopinions/opinion-24-1/.

35 New York State Bar Association Task Force on Artificial Intelligence, *Report and Recommendations of the New York State Bar Association Task Force on Artificial Intelligence*, 6 April 2024. See: https://nysba.org/wp-content/uploads/2022/03/2024-April-Report-and-Recommendations-of-the-Task-Force-on-Artificial-Intelligence.pdf.

36 American Bar Association Standing Committee on Ethics and Professional Responsibility, *Formal Opinion 512: Generative Artificial Intelligence Tools*, 29 July 2024. See: https://www.americanbar.org/news/abanews/aba-news-archives/2024/07/aba-issues-first-ethics-guidance-ai-tools/.

37 Ambrogi RJ, "Legal AI Tools Show Promise in First-of-its-Kind Benchmark Study, with Harvey and CoCounsel Leading the Pack", LawSites, 28 February 2025. See: https://www.lawnext.com/2025/02/legal-ai-tools-show-promise-in-first-of-its-kind-benchmark-study-with-harvey-and-cocounsel-leading-the-pack.html.

Chapter 5:

The legal operations leader: Designing modern legal service delivery

By Katie Moon, head of legal design and operations, and Daniel Solomon, portfolio lead: client collaboration, Lewis Silkin LLP

It is 5pm on a mid-winter Friday. An in-house lawyer is just finishing off their work for the week. Suddenly – ping! – an email arrives: "Can you share our NDA with me? It is urgent for a meeting Monday morning." The lawyer sighs. It is a quick job, they tell themselves.

At 5:03pm, another email comes through – this time, from the CEO: "I have a meeting first thing Monday re a potential new acquisition. Can you review any legal hurdles we may face before the meeting?"

At 5:07pm, a Teams message from the procurement team lands: "We need this contract reviewed for a new bit of technology as soon as possible."

The weekend, so close just a few minutes ago, now seems so far away. The lawyer is left dreaming of a world where there is more structure for requesting legal support, and where they are not viewed as the sole bottleneck for keeping business moving. This scenario is typical of the daily struggle of in-house teams: constant firefighting; shifting priorities; managing both day-to-day and outsourced work; and being seen as a blocker when legal approval is required prior to action. The team has two options: (1) hire more people, which comes with its own challenges; or (2) identify how they can better manage their time.

This is where legal operations can put a structure in place to help teams thrive. It is a discipline that takes stock and plans for the future; a discipline of doers working across the business to turn vision into reality. Legal operations professionals look at the people, processes, data, and technology used by in-house teams to deliver meaningful solutions for change and optimization. In any walk of life, a team of superstars needs glue to support the structure. Legal operations acts as that glue.

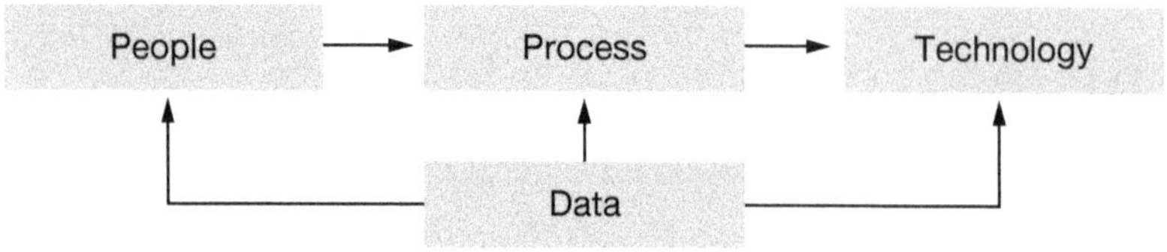

Figure 1: What legal operations professionals assess

The rise of legal operations

The purpose of a general operations function is to examine how business departments work together; how efficient processes are; and how technology can be leveraged for certain tasks, all with a view to ensuring a seamless way of working. In recent years, there has been increasing pressure on in-house legal functions to do more with less budget and headcount.[1] This growing problem has opened the pathway for legal operations. It takes the same principles as any operations function, but directs its energy towards examining and improving how an in-house legal function works.

Legal operations professionals assess different limbs of an in-house legal function to determine where points of friction lie; where there are gaps in a process or materials available; and which tasks continue to take up an exorbitant amount of time. After analyzing these pain points, processes can be redesigned to ensure the function is dedicating time to the most important and strategic work, delivering it efficiently and facilitating easier collaboration with internal stakeholders and external providers.

Not only are legal operations functions becoming more valuable within companies to meet the "do more with less" mandate, but they are also being offered as a new service within private practice. The transformative projects that legal operations experts undertake can be time-intensive and require a range of skillsets not traditionally associated with lawyers. Rather than trying to complete a project side-of-desk, in-house legal functions are turning towards law firms to support them with their legal operations initiatives and outsourcing this new type of work.

The new client-facing service of legal operations should be viewed alongside the impact of alternative legal service providers (ALSPs) and the entry of top consultancies into the legal market. One of these two players' key differentiators was their ability to equip professionals with a different skillset and provide transformative projects for in-house legal teams using value-based – rather than time-based – pricing. This allowed them to bring together people, data, process, and technology expertise, which, in turn, meant that they were able to enter the market with innovative methods of delivery. In-house teams turn to ALSPs mainly for cost reasons on volume work or for specialized work streams, such as eDisclosure.[2]

Law firms have embraced this challenge, partnering with ALSPs, where appropriate, or introducing new practice groups of legal operations professionals to provide this new offering to their clients. It is no secret that law firms are under pressure to evolve the ways in which they offer legal services and demonstrate their value to clients, in order to keep them coming back. Alongside complex legal matters, transformative legal operations projects are also being outsourced to private practice firms. These new services offer a way for law firms to holistically support their clients with operationally complex projects, which in-house teams do not have the time, headspace, or skills to do themselves.

What is the focus of legal operations?

The purpose of legal operations is to ensure that legal templates, processes, guidance materials, and other operations are working smoothly. An optimized legal function prioritizes:

- The delegation of low-risk and low-value matters to business teams by enabling self-service within clear guardrails;
- The retention of strategic matters by the in-house legal team, where detailed knowledge of the business and its objectives is crucial; and
- The outsourcing of time-draining matters to a range of legal service providers (such as ALSPs for high-volume matters that are business-as-usual or particularly complex matters to law firms).

As the aim is to ensure that a legal process works for all impacted individuals, legal operations experts work with multiple functions in a company and connect usually siloed teams, such as legal, finance, IT, procurement, marketing, compliance, and HR. They can also help in-house legal teams demonstrate their value to the company beyond anecdotes by building frameworks to provide metrics and evidence to senior leadership on how a legal team is:

- Decreasing matter cycle times;
- Enabling business self-service;
- Reducing outside counsel spend;
- Spending their time by providing transparency around their workload; and
- Saving time by leveraging technology.

Who are legal operations professionals?

Legal operations is an area that attracts people both with and without legal qualifications, creating a varied skillset and a range of backgrounds within the discipline. Some lawyers make a career change from providing pure legal advice to an operations-based role, where their firsthand knowledge and experience of being part of a process are invaluable to determining where things go wrong and how it can be improved. Others who are just starting their career in law may do some paralegal work or make it through a training contract, only to find that the day-to-day work of a lawyer is not right for them. Legal operations provides a place to apply skillsets not traditionally associated with lawyers, while allowing these professionals to stay in the field of law.

Certain law firms, such as Slaughter and May and Norton Rose Fulbright, have dedicated Legal Operations Graduate Schemes for individuals just starting their career in law, as an alternative route to the traditional training contract. As a result, there is now a much greater diversity in the roles and career paths being offered at law firms, including roles for technology specialists who are focused on legal operations. Alternatively, a legal operations professional may not have a legal background at all and enter the legal industry after gaining experience with project management, process design, technology, and change management.

In general, some of the basic skills that are required for a legal operations specialist include:

- *Adaptability:* Legal operations professionals adopt a consultative approach and therefore need to understand systems and processes used by individual clients – some of which they might not be familiar with at the outset and need to learn in a very short space of time to deliver an effective outcome.
- *Creativity:* Legal operations often requires reviewing disparate components of a process and bringing them together – for example, identifying where an existing piece of technology can be repurposed or reconfigured to meet a specific need for an in-house legal team, instead of purchasing a brand-new solution. This allows legal functions to save costs and tap into the technologies already in use by their company and, in turn, benefit from higher rates of engagement with a new process, as teams will have greater familiarity with the tool it underpins.
- *Agility:* After understanding the details of how an in-house function currently operates, the role of a legal operations professional is to then build an optimized operating model that works in the context of a

client's business. Often, it is an iterative process that requires multiple rounds of testing, refinement, and redesign to ensure any new process will meet both legal and impacted business functions' requirements.

- *Entrepreneurialism:* Legal operations is an emerging discipline for many firms. In order to build legal operations into a revenue-generating practice group, internal and external advocacy of the discipline is required to educate colleagues and clients of the power of legal operations.

What type of work do they do?

The key functions of legal operations are broken down into 12 streams[3] by the Corporate Legal Operations Consortium (CLOC), each of which is key to improving legal operations and creating a more efficient, scalable and cost-effective legal function.

Figure 2: CLOC's Core 12 framework

Within those 12 streams, there are a variety of projects and solutions that a legal operations professional can develop to improve the legal function's ways of working. These include the following.

Process mapping

- *Review:* The first step is to use a framework (such as CLOC's) to review what is happening across the legal function. Legal operations professionals do this by leading discovery workshops with those impacted by a particular process (for example, the in-house legal team and members of other affected business functions) to work through the current state of things and identify what is working well or what is missing from a process. Gathering a range of perspectives from these workshops is crucial and will inform the ways in which an issue can be resolved and how changes to the current state should be managed.
- *Mapping:* By taking information learned from those discovery workshops, an end-to-end process map is created to identify each step and decision involved in a process. This can highlight the time drains, doubled effort, confusion, and other inefficiencies that are resulting from a broken process.
- *Redesign:* Legal operations experts would then redesign the process into a future-state model by reorganizing the steps involved and updating them to increase efficiency. This could involve creating reference materials or new templates to enable self-service, leveraging technology to automate a task, or introducing new checkpoints to ensure a task is collaborative and receives required input from other teams at the right time. This future-state process map provides a blueprint of how a process can be improved, which can then be implemented.

Intake and matter management

- *The problem:* Many in-house legal teams face disorganization in how they receive, triage, manage, and deliver requests from the business. From email to Slack or Teams to text messages and watercooler chats, requests can land with the legal function in many different ways, and may lack the structure or context to enable lawyers to start work.
- *The solution*: A dedicated intake and matter management system can alleviate the confusion, disorganization, and a lack of transparency about what a legal team is working on and when a business requestor

can expect a response. There are a range of legal technology tools available that can deliver this exact framework, including Juro, Ironclad, Leah, or Icertis. However, if a legal function does not have the budget to invest in legal-specific technology, some in-house legal teams have repurposed platforms already in use by their business to act as their "legal front door". Jira, Asana, monday.com, and other general workflow management tools can be adapted as ticketing and automatic triage platforms to streamline this process for in-house legal functions.

- *The specialist's role:* Legal operations experts can map the existing process for intake and matter management to pinpoint areas for improvement; identify what types of technology and changes in the process would solve these issues; configure the new system (collaborating with technology teams as required); and provide change management support to ensure the new process can be easily adopted and resolves the original pain point.

Contract automation

Contract automation is a way to help improve contracting processes for in-house legal teams. There are different steps in the contract lifecycle which can be automated, including the initial population of a template with variable details. For example, a business stakeholder can enter a platform and complete a form which asks for basic details about their contract (such as party details, fees and contract duration). The responses provided are then automatically inserted into the contract template, producing a fully populated template for the business stakeholder, which they can share directly with their counterparty.

The introduction of artificial intelligence (AI) has added another layer to this, with automation technologies now able to extract information from documents, such as Heads of Terms, and use this to pre-populate certain fields in an automation form. When done well, contract automation saves a substantial amount of time for legal teams, as it empowers the business to create contracts quickly using the most up-to-date version (rather than using another contract as a base), with no missed fields and a reduced risk of manual errors.

However, contract automation is not necessarily a quick-win project, which is why legal operations professionals at law firms are more frequently tasked with implementing this for in-house clients. Legal operations teams support contract automation projects in the following ways:

- *Readiness:* Legal operations experts must first work with clients to determine which contract types are appropriate for self-service; whether controls should be put in place to require legal review and input before it is shared externally; and ensure the chosen templates are compatible with automation (such as by simplifying the wording and structure to ensure ease of population).
- *Implementation:* When building back-end automation workflows, legal operations professionals may collaborate with technology teams to outline the relevant automation questions and mechanics for how the form should work and flow internally. For example, internal approval might be required if the contract is above a certain value. The contract can be automatically routed internally based on responses provided in the initial form, before the contract is fully populated and ready to be shared externally.
- *Testing:* Beta testing new processes, particularly when introducing technology, is a crucial step before sending it out into the wild. Legal operations experts can run workshops with end-users (such as legal teams, business teams and approvers who will be involved in the process) and refine the automation as needed, bridging the gap between the legal and technical sides of document automation. This enables specialists to hand over a fully built and fit-for-purpose automated contract to their in-house clients, which they will be able to start using immediately.

Contract management

Legal operations professionals can also help clients unlock the information contained within their contracts by building searchable contract repositories. This can provide clients with a database of past deals that can be used to support future work and internal decisions.

- *Data extraction:* Legal operations experts can work with clients to identify which data points should be surfaced and prompt their AI tool of choice to extract these from their contracts, as opposed to manually reviewing each contract and populating the database. Pre-2022, using AI for this purpose required training and numerous examples, whereas the most recent wave of AI platforms only require a natural language prompt, making this type of project much more efficient to complete.
- *Automatic reminders:* Automated workflows can also be built into contract repositories to ensure notifications are automatically sent to

the legal team or contract owners responsible for managing certain obligations or key dates contained in a contract.

- *Contracting positions:* Depending on the type of contract terms extracted in a client's database, legal operations teams can also work with clients to review the positions they have ultimately agreed to in order to assess: (1) what standard positions the client should take as a starting point in a contract; (2) what fallback positions they would be comfortable agreeing to; and (3) what deviations would trigger an internal escalation and approvals process. These can be documented to create negotiation playbooks for legal teams (or business teams, in some instances) to standardize their approach to negotiations, ensure greater consistency in their contract portfolio, and reduce the time spent negotiating contracts.

How else is AI impacting this role?

Introducing AI into their own operations is high on an in-house team's agenda. Repeatable, high-volume tasks that previously would have been outsourced can now be done quickly and easily using AI. Tools like Harvey, Legora, Co-Counsel, and Wordsmith have been widely adopted by the legal sector, developing new legal use cases for AI every day.

In the world of AI, legal operations becomes even more important. As AI stacks become increasingly powerful and more embedded within organizations, growing emphasis is thereby placed on redefining existing processes and ripping up current ways of doing things, in order to introduce and embed AI-driven processes. Good legal operation professionals help achieve this in a structured and cohesive way, ensuring that processes are robust and long-lasting. As such, AI is increasingly providing an exciting and sustainable opportunity for legal operations teams.

New service opportunities

Legal operations teams are being engaged to support in-house legal teams with selecting, implementing, and getting the most out of AI tools. With a plethora of vendors on the market, it can be an overwhelming and daunting task for a time-poor in-house lawyer to thoroughly assess, demo, and set up a new tech tool that will effectively meet their requirements.

- *Selection:* In-house teams are turning to law firms for their views on which tools similar in-house teams are using with success, to cut through the noise and narrow down the initial pool. Furthermore, legal operations teams can work with in-house clients to identify use cases for AI and define their specific requirements. By formalizing this into a proper request for proposal (RFP) and leveraging their industry-wide knowledge, legal operations teams can help ensure that clients select the right tool or blend of tools for their needs, reducing the risk of wasted spend.

- *Readiness and implementation:* Once a tool is selected, readiness, implementation, and change management phases can be run by legal operations specialists on behalf of their clients, to ensure they are set up for success. Depending on the tool and use case, it can take months before it is fully up and running. Allowing legal operations professionals to deal with the complexities of implementation in a methodical way can allow clients to hit the ground running with their investment once it is rolled out.
- *Return on investment:* Due to the sheer volume of use cases, defining the return on investment of AI tools can be difficult, as traditional methods of tracking a return on investment do not necessarily apply. Legal operations teams are being engaged to develop more appropriate methods of understanding the value of AI investment (such as insourcing value, process enhancements, or wider legal spend), which in-house legal teams can then use internally.

Improved service delivery

As with traditional private practice lawyers using AI to analyze and report on a high volume of documents, legal operations professionals can leverage AI in a similar way:

- *Process mapping:* When redesigning processes, there may be multiple documents to sift through, all of which contain information about certain aspects of the process and may contain conflicting instructions. Using AI, all documents can be instantaneously reviewed and summarized to produce an initial draft of a process map. This saves hours of time meticulously piecing together a fragmented puzzle, allowing legal operations experts to focus on the more analytical elements of spotting and redesigning inefficiencies. The nuances that specialists will have learned during workshops, and the ability to apply an empathetic lens in relation to how changes in a process will impact the people involved, are things that AI has yet to mimic.
- *Document development:* AI can remove the "blank sheet" problem

many people face when drafting a document from scratch by creating a starting point for certain materials. For example, AI can be leveraged to identify commonly negotiated clauses across a pool of contracts and what positions are ultimately agreed to. Going one step further, tools such as Harvey, Legora, and Luminance can ingest recently negotiated contracts and use these to create a first pass of a negotiation playbook. While this should never be the endpoint, it does provide a helpful starter for legal operations experts. They can then use their skillsets to refine the AI output by creating more robust fallback positions or adapting positions based on client nuances.

- *Innovative pricing:* Embracing AI when delivering legal operations services has led to value-based pricing being more of a viable model for law firms. This lends itself well to the type of work that legal operations teams do, by leveraging a combination of their knowledge and expertise with AI to support legal teams. Taking the AI-powered playbook example, the value a client will derive from it will be through the ongoing use and predictable output of the playbook, as well as the ability to keep more work in-house. As such, the traditional hourly rate to build, test, and finalize this type of playbook is not entirely appropriate.
- *Change management:* Using AI to support in some of the ways outlined above will also give legal operations teams more time and headspace to focus on more of the strategic elements of change management. This helps ensure that the processes and solutions being implemented will stick, creating tailored materials for the end users to boost adoption.

While AI adds substantial value to the role of a legal operations specialist, it is not a silver bullet. Anyone using AI to support legal work should always make sure that they are verifying the output. Legal operations teams (and firms more generally) should not be afraid to experiment, but should always be conscious that AI can be prone to producing confident hallucinations. This should not put people off using AI in their day-to-day work, but instead should serve as a warning to avoid complacency.

From a legal operations perspective, examples of verification might mean checking the citations provided from document extraction to ensure that the tool has correctly interpreted the prompt, reviewing figures provided in AI generated reporting, or checking and refining playbook rules. To get the best outcome from using AI, it is critical to iterate by continuously refining prompting, testing new features, and stress-testing workflows and assets that are built via AI.

How will the role evolve?

The role of a legal operations expert is becoming more defined within law firms, alongside that of the traditional fee-earning lawyer, to help deliver work more seamlessly and holistically for clients. Previously, professionals with the relevant legal operations skillset were employed in discrete disciplines, such as legal project managers; business analysts; change managers; pricing specialists; and legal technologists. While present in law firms, these roles were typically internally facing or working in a non-chargeable capacity on client matters. While these internally-facing roles will not disappear, there is now a shift occurring towards these roles becoming more client-facing. Law firms that are building multidisciplinary, client-facing teams will ensure that legal operations experts can work collaboratively with lawyers to deliver an offering to clients that meets every need. The evolution of legal operations will see clients no longer engaging law firms to draft a one-off contract but, rather, to help them operationalize the use of that contract with a seamless process around it.

This also points to another evolution in legal operations – from moving beyond pure consultative work to hands-on implementation. Clients outsource complex matters to law firms because of the lack of time and expertise to get it done; similarly, in-house teams will outsource large, transformative projects to law firms to take the heavy lifting off their desk. Recommendations reports on how clients can improve their ways of working will no longer cut it – clients will increasingly ask for hands-on support to implement a legal operations project roadmap. To effectively build this new service offering, law firms will need to:

1. *Spot opportunities with current work:* Law firms should begin by analyzing how they currently support their clients and consider how they could incorporate some of the innovative and transformative work that legal operations specialists thrive in. Having an internal workshop to map opportunities can ensure a firm develops this offering in line with its existing capabilities.
2. *Prove the concept:* As with any new product or service, legal operations services can initially be provided to clients as a value-add. For example, a law firm working with a client on a discrete part of a broader

contracting process could take the opportunity to proactively identify a client's operational pain point and recommend ways in which the process could be streamlined. This can help to establish whether there is a client demand for this type of service and enable the firm to begin building credibility around solving these types of problems for clients. It also helps the firm learn lessons and iterate as they look to build standardized methodologies and materials.

3. *Productize:* Once initial credentials are in place, the firm can begin productizing this offering as a standalone, revenue-generating service. This can be organic growth stemming from work already completed with clients, but gradually developing into more tailored, complex solutions which busy in-house legal or legal operations functions simply do not have time to do thoroughly.

Ultimately, the role of a legal operations professional within private practice will evolve in line with market demand. More and more companies are trending towards building out their own in-house legal operations teams and, as this continues, it will essentially open a new target market for law firms. Not only will traditional in-house legal teams be a target clientele, but so too will in-house legal operations teams.

References

1 Thomson Reuters Institute and Buying Legal Council, 2025 Legal Department Operations Index: Managing pressures both external and internal, Thomson Reuters, 2025. See: https://legalsolutions.thomsonreuters.co.uk/content/dam/ewp-m/documents/legal/en/pdf/reports/legal-department-operations-index-report.pdf?

2 Thomson Reuters Institute, the Center on Ethics and the Legal Profession at Georgetown Law and the Professional Service Firms (PSF) Group at Saïd Business School, University of Oxford, *Alternative Legal Services Providers 2025: Strong growth amid signs of a bifurcating market*, Thomson Reuters, 2025. See: https://www.thomsonreuters.com/en-us/posts/wp-content/uploads/sites/20/2025/01/ALSP-Report-2025.pdf.

3 Corporate Legal Operations Consortium, "CLOC's Core 12 framework guides and supports operational excellence", 2026. See: https://cloc.org/cloc-core-12/.

Chapter 6:
AI governance professionals: Managing risk in the AI-enabled law firm

By Harry Borovick, general counsel, Luminance, and Amy Merrick, senior legal counsel, Google DeepMind

A senior associate at a mid-sized commercial firm pastes a privileged interview memo into a third-party summarization tool. The tool is not on the firm's approved list and is a free-to-use open version of the tool. No one reviews the output. The summary – stripped of nuance and missing a critical qualifier – finds its way into a client briefing note. The client's opponent later raises questions about how the document was produced and argues that it is no longer privileged. The firm has no audit trail; no record of what entered the tool; and no policy that covers the scenario.

Nothing here involves a dramatic failure of artificial intelligence (AI). The tool did roughly what it was asked to do. The failure was organizational: the firm had an approved list, but no one had decided who could use which tools, on which data, or under what review standard. The technology worked; the governance did not exist.

That gap between AI capability and institutional control is why AI governance professionals are emerging inside law firms. Their job is not to slow adoption down. It is to make adoption structured, reviewable, and defensible.

Why governance roles are emerging now

AI typically enters a law firm as a productivity story. A partner wants a drafting copilot; an associate wants faster research; or business services want document summarization or workflow automation. *Everyone* wants less friction for time recording and billing. However, almost immediately, the productivity story becomes a governance story. The questions start being asked: can client material be uploaded? Is the tool approved? Will prompts be retained? Who verifies the output? What do we tell clients?

Traditional legal technology supported the work *around* legal judgment: storing documents, managing matters, tracking time. Increasingly, AI systems are being used not simply to support legal work, but to perform tasks that previously required lawyer judgment, particularly for lower-value, repetitive matters. Generative AI is closer to the work product itself: it drafts. In a profession in which technological competence is increasingly recognized as a professional duty, using new tools without proper governance increases the firm's overall risk exposure. This risk stems not from the inherent nature of the technology, but from a failure to manage how it is used.[1]

The risk extends well beyond "hallucinations". A firm's AI posture now touches client confidentiality, privilege, personal data, record retention, cybersecurity, and vendor dependency. The American Bar Association's (ABA) Formal Opinion 512 put it plainly: a lawyer's duties of competence, confidentiality, and communication all apply when generative AI is used in legal practice, and the lawyer remains responsible for the output, regardless of how it was produced.[2]

Law firms also face a distinctly matter-based governance challenge. A firm may approve a tool in principle, yet a specific client may prohibit external models, require local hosting, or impose contractual restrictions on data handling. Governance must work at two levels: a firm-wide baseline and matter-specific overlays.

Blanket bans rarely solve the problem. One 2024 industry survey found that 79 percent of lawyers reported using generative AI at work, yet many did so without formal guidance from their firms.[3] This type of "shadow" AI grows when the sanctioned path is too slow, vague, or difficult. Good governance is specific and proportionate to the organization; it emerges because firms need something more sophisticated than either uncontrolled experimentation or total prohibition.

Clients are accelerating this shift. They may want to know what tools are used; whether their data train models; how outputs are reviewed; and how the firm would respond if something went wrong. Governance is becoming part of client service. However, plenty of clients are simply happy to trust their counsel to use the right tools for the job. After all, the risk of breaching engagement terms, data protection obligations, or professional duties, and the liability that follows under professional indemnity insurance rests with the firm.

The governance professional as translator

The common thread across AI governance roles is translation. The best governance professionals understand enough law to appreciate confidentiality, privilege, and client obligations; enough technology to understand models, integrations, and logging; and enough about delivery operations to know how lawyers actually work under pressure. Their day-to-day work is foundational:

- Maintaining an inventory of AI use cases and classifying them by risk;
- Reviewing vendors against security, privacy, and professional responsibility requirements;
- Defining documentation, retention, and audit standards;
- Designing approval gates and coordinating incident response;
- Drafting client-facing position statements and supporting procurement questionnaires; and
- Ensuring each tool, and each meaningful use case, has an owner.

They ask the questions that make AI usable at scale: what problem is this solving? What data enters it? What leaves it? What human judgment remains? What would we need to prove later? These questions are not friction for their own sake; they are what turn experimentation into institutional capability.

A practical risk framework: The "four gates"

The best governance frameworks are simple enough for busy lawyers to follow and robust enough for risk teams to defend. One useful structure is a four-gate model, adapted from broader AI risk management principles, such as the National Institute of Standards and Technology's *Artificial Intelligence Risk Management Framework*.[4]

1. Can this tool enter the firm?

Governance professionals need to look beyond marketing language and understand the architecture:

- *Data handling:* Does the vendor retain prompts or outputs? Are customer data used for training?
- *Security controls:* What encryption, segregation, deletion, and audit log capabilities exist? Which subprocessors are involved?
- *Identity and access:* How are permissions managed? What happens upon termination?
- *Change notification:* How will the vendor notify customers of changes to the model or product behavior?

Every approved tool should have an identified business owner, an intended use profile, and clear conditions of use. Without these, the firm has not approved a tool – it has approved ambiguity. Firms should also consider maintaining a diverse AI register with multiple approved options, so that lawyers can select the right tool for the job. Different tools may have different strengths – in jurisdictional coverage, training data sources, or task suitability – and a register that makes these distinctions visible will aid both faster adoption and better-informed use.

2. Can it touch this matter?

An approved tool is not approved for every task or matter. This gate introduces risk tiering based on four questions: how sensitive are the data, how material is the task, where will the output go, and what client-specific restrictions apply?

Low-risk internal tasks may be pre-approved. Higher-risk uses may require a private environment, enhanced review, or explicit client permission. For example, using an approved tool to summarize publicly available regulatory guidance for an internal knowledge brief is a different proposition from uploading a draft merger agreement into the same tool for clause analysis. A client engaged on a cross-border sanctions matter may contractually prohibit the use of any AI tool hosted outside a specific jurisdiction. Firms need a way to capture the purpose, owner, matter context, data categories, and retention rules for AI-enabled workflows – whether in a use-case register or a matter-specific governance record.

Prompts and output may become part of the matter history. Some may need to be retained, others deleted, and others carefully excluded. Governance professionals decide what becomes a record, what remains ephemeral, and how those decisions align with client obligations.

3. Can the output leave human control?

The core rule is: AI supports judgment; it does not replace accountability. No material output should reach a client, a counterparty, or a court without human review by someone competent to check it. "Material" here means any task requiring the exercise of legal judgment or producing content on which a client or third party will rely. Non-material tasks – formatting a document, generating a first-pass timeline from undisputed dates, or drafting internal meeting notes – may carry a lighter review burden, but even these require a lawyer's oversight where privileged or confidential information is involved, to ensure that the mere act of processing does not compromise the privilege itself. In *Mata v. Avianca, Inc.*, two lawyers were sanctioned for filing a brief containing fabricated case citations generated by ChatGPT.[5] In the UK, the Upper Tribunal emphasized in *Hamid* that legal professionals "are expected to ensure that such documents are checked [and] that errors are identified", and that failure to do so could result in serious disciplinary consequences.[6]

Firms also need to distinguish between decision support and autonomous action. A tool that *proposes* language is one thing; an agent or series of agents that sends emails, updates systems, or files documents is quite another. The practical test is: can the responsible lawyer understand, explain, and defend how the result was produced?

4. What happens when the tool changes?

Approval is not a one-time event: vendors update models; agentic functionality may be switched on. Governance professionals need a process for reviewing release notes; authority to pause usage when a change introduces unacceptable risk; version tracking; and benchmark tests to detect behavioral drift. They should also consider the currency of the tool's underlying data: is the model retrained on the client's own work product, on publicly available legal materials, or on a curated dataset? How frequently are that data refreshed, and how does the firm satisfy itself that the tool reflects current law and market practice, rather than outdated precedent?

Across all four gates, auditability is the dividing line between governance and wishful thinking. Every material use case should leave enough evidence to reconstruct what happened: the tool and version, the user, the matter context, the human reviewer, and the key decisions taken. Near-misses should change the workflow, not just trigger a reminder.

The privilege question: When AI meets confidentiality

Of all the risks that AI introduces into legal practice, the potential compromise of legal professional privilege may be the most consequential. In February 2026, two US federal courts addressed generative AI in the privilege context for the first time. Weeks later, the Upper Tribunal in England delivered its own ruling on the same question. Together, these decisions mark a turning point: the relationship between AI tools and legal privilege is no longer a matter of speculation.

United States v. Heppner: Privilege denied

In *United States v. Heppner*,[7] a financial services executive charged with securities fraud used Anthropic's Claude – a publicly available generative AI assistant – to create 31 documents analyzing his legal position and outlining defense strategy. He later shared these documents with his lawyers. When the government sought their production, the defendant claimed both attorney–client privilege and work product protection.

Judge Rakoff rejected both claims. The court held that the essential elements of attorney–client privilege were absent: the AI chatbot was not the defendant's attorney; the communications were not made for the purpose of obtaining legal advice from counsel; and the exchange was not confidential. On this last point, the court emphasized that Anthropic's terms of service expressly permitted the collection and use of inputs and outputs, including disclosure to "governmental regulatory authorities".[8] The defendant could not have had a reasonable expectation of privacy.

The work product claim also failed. The documents were not prepared at the direction of counsel. As the court observed, the AI tool "might arguably be said to have functioned in a manner akin to a highly trained professional who may act as a lawyer's agent", had counsel directed the exchange. However, that was not what happened.[9] The judge concluded:

> *Generative artificial intelligence presents a new frontier in the ongoing dialogue between technology and the law. Time will tell whether, as in the case of other technological advances, generative artificial intelligence will fulfil its promise to revolutionize the way we process information. But AI's novelty does not mean that its use is not subject to longstanding legal principles, such as those governing the attorney–client privilege.*

Warner v. Gilbarco: A contrasting result

Decided in the same month, *Warner v. Gilbarco* reached a different outcome on work product protection.[10] A *pro se* litigant in the Eastern District of Michigan used a public AI platform to assist with legal analysis after the close of discovery. The court held that the materials were protected work product, because they reflected the plaintiff's own mental impressions prepared in anticipation of litigation. On the question of waiver, the court concluded that disclosure to a public AI platform did not meaningfully increase the likelihood that the material would reach an adversary, and that generative AI programs are "tools, not persons".[11]

The Sidley Austin analysis of these decisions is instructive: *Heppner* treats AI as potentially agent-like when used at counsel's direction, while *Warner* treats AI as a neutral instrument for waiver purposes.[12] As generative AI becomes more autonomous and embedded in litigation workflows, how courts resolve this "tool versus agent" tension will have significant implications for firms.

Hamid: The UK position crystallizes

In *UK v. Secretary of State for the Home Department* [2026] UKUT 81 (*Hamid*), the Upper Tribunal addressed AI and privilege in the context of an immigration solicitor who had uploaded client correspondence and Home Office decision letters into ChatGPT for the purpose of making summaries – an administrative task, not legal drafting. The Tribunal stated:

> *To put client letters and decision letters from the Home Office into an open-source AI tool … is to place this information on the internet in the public domain, and thus to breach client confidentiality and waive legal privilege.*

The Tribunal drew a distinction between "open-source" tools, such as ChatGPT, and "closed source," tools such as Microsoft Copilot, noting that the latter "do not place information in the public domain" and are available for summarization "without these risks". However, as several commentators have noted, the Tribunal's reasoning is thin. It did not examine the AI provider's terms of service or explain the basis for the open/closed distinction.[13] The ruling nonetheless aligns with judicial guidance issued by the Courts and Tribunals Judiciary in October 2025, which warned that "any information that you input into a public AI chatbot should be seen as being published to all the world".[14]

The practical consequence is stark. Norton Rose Fulbright has observed: "If privilege over a document is waived by the use of an open-source AI tool, it is no different to waiver by other means: i.e., there is no mechanism by which privilege can be retrospectively asserted or recovered."[15]

AI notetakers and the expanding perimeter

The risk is not limited to text-based AI tools. AI-powered notetakers that record and transcribe meetings present a distinct vector. As CMS has noted, unlike email servers or conferencing platforms that merely carry a communication, AI notetakers "process its substance and produce derivative work product, often under terms that allow the provider to use the data to improve its systems".[16] The 2025 US case of *Brewer v. Otter.ai Inc.* raised allegations that an AI notetaker intercepted meeting content of non-users and used conversation data to train machine learning models without adequate consent.[17] Firms that permit AI notetakers on privileged calls without examining the provider's terms face the same waiver risk.

Practical implications for governance

These decisions crystallize several governance imperatives:

- *Vendor due diligence must address privilege explicitly.* The *Heppner* court's analysis turned on the platform's terms of service. Governance teams must review whether the vendor retains input, uses them for training, or reserves the right to disclose them to third parties. Teams should also establish whether the vendor can review prompts or outputs for its own purposes – for example, product improvement, model fine-tuning, or monitoring for terms-of-service violations such as harmful content – and whether such access is compatible with the firm's confidentiality obligations.
- *The consumer/enterprise distinction is now a legal requirement, not a preference.* Both *Hamid* and the judicial guidance draw a clear line between public-facing tools and closed enterprise systems. Firms must enforce that distinction through policy, technical controls, and training.
- *Counsel direction matters. Heppner* left open the possibility that privilege might attach if AI is used at counsel's direction within a confidential environment. Governance frameworks should capture whether AI use on a matter is directed, supervised, and documented by counsel.
- *Administrative uses are not exempt.* The solicitor in *Hamid* was summarizing decision letters, not drafting legal submissions. The privilege risk attaches to any input of confidential material, regardless of the task; and
- *Incident response must cover privilege compromise.* Once privileged material enters a public AI tool, there may be no mechanism to recover the privilege. Firms need a clear protocol: vendor notification, deletion requests, client notification, and regulatory self-reporting where appropriate.
- *Client-generated AI drafts raise their own privilege questions.* Where a non-lawyer client uses their company's enterprise AI to draft a legal document and then asks outside counsel to review it, the privilege analysis may differ from conventional instruction. The document was

not prepared at the direction of counsel, and the AI tool's terms of service may not satisfy the confidentiality requirements for privilege to attach. Firms should be alert to this scenario and consider whether to advise clients on it proactively.

Cybersecurity, client assurance, and the new trust question

In the AI-enabled law firm, cybersecurity and AI governance are converging. Familiar principles still matter: privilege, access control, segregation, encryption, incident response. However, generative AI introduces new failure modes: prompt leakage (where confidential inputs are inadvertently exposed through model behavior); shadow AI (unauthorized use of unapproved tools); unsafe connectors (integrations that pass data to third-party services without adequate controls); prompt injection (where a malicious input manipulates the model into producing unintended outputs); cross-tenant exposure (where one customer's data become visible to another); and opaque subprocessors (downstream service providers whose data handling cannot be verified by the firm).[18] In an agentic environment, the risk is not only bad text – it is bad actions.

The modern client assurance conversation is no longer "Do you use AI?" Rather, it is: "Under what conditions do you use it? Which data can enter it? How are outputs reviewed? What can the vendor do with our information?" Law firm clients are increasingly incorporating AI-specific questions into their security assessments and outside counsel guidelines.[19] This trend will accelerate as in-house legal teams develop their own AI governance maturity and benchmark outside counsel against it.

Governance professionals translate technical reality into client-trustworthy assurance. They create baseline statements about approved tools, prohibited practices, review standards, and escalation routes. In legal services, security is not just a technical condition – it is a trust condition. A firm that cannot explain its AI controls will sound unprepared. A firm that can explain them clearly will sound disciplined and safe to work with.

Governance as a competitive advantage

At first glance, governance looks like overhead; in practice, it is an adoption engine. Firms adopt AI faster when lawyers know what is safe and what is prohibited. Innovation teams move faster when low-risk uses have pre-approved pathways. Clients are more receptive when the firm can explain its guardrails in plain language.

The most effective governance functions reduce decision latency for routine matters and concentrate scrutiny where the stakes are highest. They create safe defaults, usable rules, and escalation paths that people actually follow. In doing so, they reduce shadow AI, tool sprawl, and unproductive arguments about edge cases.

They also create repeatability. Once a firm has clear governance standards, it can roll out approved workflows across practice groups and explain quality control in ways that strengthen client value narratives. This is where "responsible AI" stops being a slogan. Responsible AI is the principles layer: fairness, accountability, transparency, security, human oversight. Governance is the operational layer that turns those principles into daily practice.

Governance also forces firms to confront an uncomfortable workforce question. If AI automates much of the "grunt work" that junior lawyers have traditionally used to develop their foundational skills and legal judgment, how do those lawyers learn to exercise – and defend – the very judgment that AI outputs require? A junior who has never manually reviewed a data room or drafted a due diligence report from scratch may struggle to spot where an AI summary has gone wrong. Governance frameworks should, therefore, address not only how AI is used, but how the next generation of lawyers is trained to oversee it. Juniors will need to be able to defend AI-assisted output to a client who asks how a particular conclusion was reached.

There is also an emerging question about the impact of AI on billing. In a multi-jurisdictional evaluation, AI can perform the initial heavy lifting across ten or more countries, with local counsel verifying the output rather than producing it from scratch – saving significant cost and bridging language barriers, particularly where the underlying legal question is relatively straightforward. Against this must be weighed the time taken to check AI output thoroughly, which for complex or novel questions may approach the time it would have taken without the tool at all. Governance professionals should help firms think honestly about where AI genuinely reduces effort and where it merely shifts it.

Mature firms track indicators such as: time to approve low-risk use cases; percentage of AI tools inventoried with an identified owner; share of client questionnaires answered from standard materials; adoption rates for approved tools versus shadow use; and turnaround time for reassessment after vendor changes. These are not vanity metrics. They show whether the firm's AI use is governable at scale.

Key takeaways

- *Governance is operational, not theoretical.* The best governance professionals are translators who move between legal duties, technical architecture, and delivery operations.
- *Use a gated framework.* Four questions structure the risk: can this tool enter the firm? Can it touch this matter? Can the output leave human control? What happens when the tool changes?
- *Privilege is now a live litigation risk. Heppner* and *Hamid* confirm that uploading privileged material to a public AI tool can waive privilege irreversibly. The consumer/enterprise distinction is a legal requirement, not a preference.
- *Auditability is non-negotiable.* Every material AI-assisted output should leave enough evidence to reconstruct how it was produced.
- *Client assurance is a new commercial differentiator.* Firms that can explain their AI controls clearly – without jargon – earn trust.
- *Governance accelerates adoption.* Safe defaults, pre-approved pathways, and usable rules reduce shadow AI and decision latency; and
- *Fix systems, not just policies.* When near misses happen, change the workflow, the permissions, and the defaults – not just the training deck.

References

1 The obligation of technological competence is recognized in 42 US jurisdictions through amendments to the American Bar Association's Model Rules of Professional Conduct, Rule 1.1, Comment [8]. In Canada, see Federation of Law Societies of Canada, *Model Code of Professional Conduct*, Rule 3.1–2, Comment [4A], as amended in 2019. In the UK, the Solicitors Regulation Authority's guidance emphasizes lawyers' existing duties of competence and supervision when using AI tools.

2 Standing Committee on Ethics and Professional Responsibility, *Formal Opinion 512: Generative Artificial Intelligence Tools*, American Bar Association, 29 July 2024. The opinion addresses duties of competence (Rule 1.1), confidentiality (Rule 1.6), communication (Rule 1.4), candor (Rule 3.3), and supervisory responsibilities (Rules 5.1–5.3).

3 Thomson Reuters, *Future of Professionals Report: AI-powered technology & the forces shaping professional work*, July 2024. See: https://www.thomsonreuters.com/content/dam/ewp-m/documents/thomsonreuters/en/pdf/reports/future-of-professionals-report-2024.pdf.

4 National Institute of Standards and Technology, *Artificial Intelligence Risk Management Framework* (AI RMF 1.0), January 2023. See: https://nvlpubs.nist.gov/nistpubs/ai/nist.ai.100-1.pdf.

5 *Mata v. Avianca, Inc.*, No. 22-cv-1461 (S.D.N.Y. 2023). Lawyers Peter LoDuca and Steven Schwartz were sanctioned after submitting a brief containing at least six fabricated case citations generated by ChatGPT.

6 *UK v. Secretary of State for the Home Department* [2026] UKUT 81 (IAC) (*Hamid*). The Upper Tribunal joined two cases involving AI-generated fictitious citations and use of consumer AI tools by immigration solicitors. On the duty to check AI outputs, see also *R (on the application of Ayinde) v. London Borough of Haringey* [2025] EWHC 1383 (Admin).

7 *United States v. Heppner*, No. 25 Cr. 00503 (JSR) (S.D.N.Y., Feb. 10, 2026).

8 Bond T, Speed J and Lanzkron L, "The status of legal professional privilege when using AI tools", Bird & Bird, 7 April 2026. See: www.twobirds.com/en/insights/2026/uk/the-status-of-legal-professional-privilege-when-using—ai-tools.

9 Hall T, Tyagi A and Todd L, "Generative AI, LLMs and AI notetakers: A new threat to legal professional privilege?", CMS, 23 February 2026. See: https://cms.law/en/gbr/legal-updates/generative-ai-llms-and-ai-notetakers-a-new-threat-to-legal-professional-privilege.

10 *Warner v. Gilbarco* (E.D. Mich., Feb. 2026). Discussed in: Gordon DA, Ono T, Jackson MS et al, "Generative AI and Privilege: Practical Lessons from Two Early Decisions and What Comes Next", Sidley Austin LLP, 3 March 2026. See: https://datamatters.sidley.com/2026/03/03/generative-ai-and-privilege-practical-lessons-from-two-early-decisions-and-what-comes-next/.

11 *Ibid.*

12 *Ibid.*

13 Bond T, Speed J and Lanzkron L, "The status of legal professional privilege when using AI tools", Bird & Bird, 7 April 2026. See: www.twobirds.com/en/insights/2026/uk/the-status-of-legal-professional-privilege-when-using--ai-tools. The authors observe that the Tribunal's open/closed distinction "raises more questions than it answers", noting that the crucial factor lies in the contractual terms governing the tool's handling of inputs and outputs, which the Tribunal did not examine.

14 Courts and Tribunals Judiciary, *Artificial Intelligence (AI): Guidance for Judicial Office Holders*, 31 October 2025. See: https://www.judiciary.uk/guidance-and-resources/artificial-intelligence-ai-judicial-guidance-october-2025/.

15 Judkins A and Vickers R, "Court guidance that use of open-source AI waives confidentiality and legal professional privilege", Norton Rose Fulbright, 9 April 2026. See: www.nortonrosefulbright.com/en/inside-disputes/blog/202604-court-guidance-that-use-of-open-source-ai-waives-confidentiality-and-legal-professional.

16 Hall T, Tyagi A and Todd L, "Generative AI, LLMs and AI notetakers: A new threat to legal professional privilege?", CMS, 23 February 2026. See: https://cms.law/en/gbr/legal-updates/generative-ai-llms-and-ai-notetakers-a-new-threat-to-legal-professional-privilege.

17 *Brewer v. Otter.ai Inc.*, Case No. 5:25-cv-06911 (N.D. Cal. 2025). Cited in: Hall T, Tyagi A and Todd L, "Generative AI, LLMs and AI notetakers: A new threat to legal professional privilege?", CMS, 23 February 2026. See: https://cms.law/en/gbr/legal-updates/generative-ai-llms-and-ai-notetakers-a-new-threat-to-legal-professional-privilege.

18 OWASP, "Top 10 for Large Language Model Applications", 2026. See: https://owasp.org/www-project-top-10-for-large-language-model-applications/.

19 International Legal Technology Association, *2024 Technology Survey*, 30 September 2024. See: https://www.iltanet.org/resources/publications/surveys/ts24.

Chapter 7: Designing the modern legal workforce: Building multidisciplinary teams for the AI-enabled law firm

By Dr Catriona Wolfenden, director of product and innovation, Weightmans LLP

The times, they are a-changin'

Ten years ago, if you had asked someone in a law firm what a multidisciplinary team looked like, you may well have received a blank look or been told that it was "innovative" for a corporate and a real estate lawyer to be working together on the same project for a client. Now, it is pleasingly less rare for a business analyst, a data specialist, a legal engineer or technologist, or any combination of those roles and others to be engaged on the same client project, at the same time, with the legal team. This is significant, because it brings an entirely different perspective to problem-solving for clients and firms: an acceptance that it is not only lawyers who are capable of having ideas that solve a particular client's problem! While it is important to understand the legal landscape behind a client's problem, this is often only one aspect of an overall solution. To find the answer or the scale of the issue for a client, you may use natural language processing (NLP) or generative artificial intelligence (genAI) to review a batch of documents. You may then use document automation (or genAI) to draft a document amendment and end up with new documents at a speed and scale that hasn't always been possible.

Why is this change important? It remains my firm view that the successful law firms of the future will be those that are able to put together multidisciplinary teams who can design solutions for clients – only part of which may need formal, traditional, legal input. This is especially the case in a world in which increasing use of and reliance on AI means that data and governance is critical.

As an introductory caveat, it is important to flag that, while (gen) AI is never far away from the legal press headlines, many innovation teams have been working successfully with different types of AI for many years. The current wave of (gen) AI is often an extension of the work that innovation teams were undertaking, offering an additional set of tech and capabilities that can be applied to particular problems. While we have seen the more recent creation of some new roles, such as prompt engineer, law firms have excelled at inventing a plethora of new titles for innovation roles over the last decade. Some firms have chosen to incorporate additional roles into innovation teams; some have added "AI" as a prefix to existing roles; others who have historically not been known for their innovation have rebranded as AI-enabled. Whatever moniker or approach is used, what matters is certain key skills should exist somewhere in your firm, whether you are starting from scratch on an innovation, AI, or product team or are merging existing functions. However you chop and change the wording, I believe the same principles apply. With that in mind, this chapter will explore the ways in which a multidisciplinary team can be curated, and some of the pitfalls you may encounter along the way.

The capabilities modern teams need

I have written elsewhere[1] about the journey Weightmans LLP embarked on to set up an innovation team from scratch. This was successful, allowing us to solve clients' problems and work with colleagues in relation to how we service legal work. While we had recruited and trained people to cultivate a wide skillset, we lacked some of the commercial abilities that roles such as a sales manager or a product manager can bring. When we evolved into a product and innovation department, we promptly started to recruit for those skills, which I will discuss later in this chapter. Our approach to setting up innovation and, subsequently, product teams is equally applicable to establishing similar departments, such as (gen) AI teams.

There has been much debate about whether lawyers need to be able to prompt (mirroring earlier debates about whether lawyers need to be able to code), and much discourse concerning the rise of prompt engineer roles in law firms and, indeed, whole departments focused on genAI. The conversation tends to go that genAI is the only thing people in law firms need to know about. In this world, the answer to everything is a hammer, so you train everyone to operate a hammer. However, this really misses the point when it comes to the purpose of innovation, which is to creatively problem-solve (and the means of doing this isn't always a hammer). In multidisciplinary teams, you naturally require technical expertise; however, in many respects, and given the pace of technological change, core skills are arguably more important. In my experience, a successful innovation team is multidisciplinary, with a mixture of the following characteristics (recognizing that people can, of course, wear multiple or differing hats, depending upon the project!).

The planners

Planning in the context of innovation may sound counterintuitive. However, while there is a fair amount of trial-and-error with innovation, planning brings necessary structure, helping a team manage multiple projects, prioritize effectively, and improve the likelihood of successful outcomes. Planners help teams anticipate challenges early and mitigate issues. Having planners in the team also supports sustainable capability-building, because it ensures a range of skills are deliberately developed and, crucially, shared.

The thinkers

Thinkers thrive in the ambiguity of innovation; they use the lack of structure to explore problems more deeply, shape strategy, and generate ideas. They add real value to exercises like premortems, where open, unconstrained thinking helps surface risks early and strengthen delivery before issues arise. However, you need to ensure that overthinking doesn't occur by balancing depth with pace, encouraging timely decisions, a broader focus, and the confidence to act with imperfect information.

The doers

These characters drive momentum, often teaching themselves new skills or tech, and join up the practical and theoretical aspects to innovation without needing to wait for total clarity. The balance to be struck here is to encourage them to maintain pace without developing tunnel vision, and it is important to ensure these team members stay open-minded to other ways of solving a particular problem.

The risk-takers

Innovation tends to attract people willing to take a risk, as many of us have moved into emerging roles from well-trodden career paths. Of course, the skill is making informed decisions about which risks are worth taking. A balance of risk appetites in the team is helpful for decision-making, preventing a default to either end of an extreme.

The rebels

It's my belief that innovation teams need a bit of rebellion – people who are willing to challenge the status quo and cut through unnecessary bureaucracy. This instinct, when used well, keeps project momentum going, but does rely on people knowing when to push and when to play the game. As teams grow, the challenge is keeping that edge without creating chaos.

The big picture people

They bring a useful perspective, helping a team avoid getting stuck in the weeds and keeping everyone focused on the overall aim. People who can see the connections across teams, clients and systems help to spot patterns and link related problems to prevent silos.

The details people

These team members' keen attention to dotting their Is and crossing their Ts is a skill that collectively benefits an innovation team, provided it is not taken to an extreme.

The people people

While innovation is "all about the people", all the people are different, so you need a broad range of people willing (or at least able) to engage, communicate, and collaborate across the business. It is useful to build the team's ability to tailor their communication styles, listen properly, and bring others with them. These skills definitely improve with practice.

While a multidisciplinary team is, in my view, not a roomful of different lawyers, there is no doubt that legal expertise is needed – ideally from a senior lawyer who understands clients and is curious and eager to try different ways of solving a particular problem. There are a very small number of these types of lawyers, who we have previously described as "gold dust lawyers", with some legendary characteristics to must be nurtured:

> *As mythical as a unicorn, the gold dust lawyer is, as the name suggests, exceptionally rare. They are the perfect mix of legal knowledge, client contact, and creative problem-solving. They are good at joining up the dots (and silos) in organizations. They are networked internally and externally as they are good with people and pleasant to work with. They know what they know and what they do not know and are keen to learn more. They understand that there are, whisper it, professionals in law firms who: (i) are not lawyers; (ii) do not want to be a lawyer; (iii) have experience in domains that the lawyers do not have; and (iv) can offer value to lawyers from other specialisms, be that HR, marketing, IT or, indeed, innovation.*[2]

Choosing the right operating model

Your existing organizational set-up will, to a large part, dictate your team structure and where innovation, AI, or product teams will sit within the overall firm. If these teams do not already exist, you have multiple options to consider, including making them standalone or part of IT, change or transformation, KM, operations, or client-facing teams.

Much will also depend upon the reporting lines you wish to establish. Our team are lucky to have been board-sponsored by our managing partner, and my role as innovation manager and then director of product and innovation reported first to a board member (the chief innovation and technology officer) and now to the firm's board client director. What is important is that innovation has been supported by the board, rather than being a nebulous concept to which lip service is paid. Although our team has been lucky to have strong sponsorship, we have also benefited from a fair amount of autonomy. While we need to collaborate with many people within our organization, innovation decisions are not made by committee. Instead, we have been given the room to succeed, empowered to work to a set of agreed objectives and let our track record speak for us (just as a lawyer would). Our board sponsorship and the fact that the product and innovation have reported to a board member have helped us to establish credibility and get buy-in from some who may otherwise have been reluctant to support. However, nothing establishes credibility like solving a problem for a client in a way that makes a lawyer look good and brings in income in a repeatable and scalable way.

Here are some common options if you are considering setting up or rearranging innovation, AI, or product teams.

A new, centralized team

This new, centralized team can sit within an existing department, such as IT, innovation, or business change. It is hard to fly the plane as you are building this new team, so this option can allow you to accelerate at some pace by piggybacking off existing infrastructures and workflows. These processes may or may not fit in the long term. If not, it can be difficult to be dispense with them – you may be told "That is how we work" or "That is what we track", so be prepared for some tricky conversations. You will also encounter the usual challenges of integrating different groups of people and changing the processes workflows of an established team.

At Weightmans, we viewed our processes as transitory and appropriate for the size of team we had or the type of work we did at any given time. They were there to evolve; if we thought of a better way of doing something, we would adjust. When we broadened the team, we used this as an opportunity to reevaluate and amend processes. In practice, how this lands depends on the social standing and internal reputation of team you are becoming a part of, which could be either a blessing or a curse. Depending upon your organizational hierarchy, there may be a question as to the level of influence you want your new team to have, and where the team may be best housed to serve this purpose if you have multiple options.

A new, centralized department

This could take the form of a standalone product, innovation, or AI function (or a combination of any or all of these). This approach allows you to be more in control of the team's destiny, processes, and ways of working; however, it is arguably the hardest option to start from scratch and deliver value at the same time. You have no track record to trade from and, depending upon how you position it, it may be seen as a "hype" or PR move.

Additionally, depending on the mix of skills and roles in the team, centralization could result in the team being disconnected from the colleagues and clients whom it is trying to solve problems for. At Weightmans, we mitigated this by introducing product and innovation partner roles (PIPs).

A non-centralized team or department

Scattering people around a firm, perhaps by aligning them to particular types of legal work or clients, offers the advantage of them being closely aligned to practice and client needs. However, it is seldom just one person who singlehandedly solves a problem and possesses all the knowledge or technical skills to be able to deliver the best solution. If you go down this route, you run the very real risk of failing to attain the best answer to every problem.

Law firms love a silo; in practice, this seldom benefits anyone. Creating multiple innovation silos risks duplication of effort at best, or – at worst – multiple workflows implemented or technology procured to solve what is, at its root, a shared problem, such as document automation. Dependency on key figures will exist, and you risk all institutional knowledge for that practice area disappearing if that person leaves. Reporting lines can also be messy: the lawyers who run existing legal teams are often not best placed to manage innovation team members.

Without some considerable effort to connect the individuals from the various practice or client groups, you are unlikely to benefit from joined-up processes or ways of reporting. At worst, there is considerable potential for this approach to overwhelm any existing teams (IT, risk, data, and so on) that many projects must work with to be successful, as each practice area will consider themselves to be the highest priority for requests made. As a result, it may fall to various other teams to attempt to prioritize all requests.

The Weightmans approach

We already had an innovation team when we looked to start a product team. When it was created, it sat within a business change department, and we initially borrowed some of their ways of working to get started before adapting them for our purposes. The business change department sat within our business services division. From the very beginning, our intention was to become a standalone department comprising people with a broad and mixed skillset. Although we work closely with many teams, including IT and business change, we consciously wanted to avoid being incorporated within those teams. When we had reached a critical mass, both in terms of numbers and success, we became a product and innovation department within the business services division and proceeded to recruit for a whole new product team to join us.

We made the decision to establish a centralized center of excellence for product and innovation (P&I) (with the same approach for a genAI department), as opposed to practice-embedded specialists. In part, this was to encourage people to think beyond a particular practice area and apply capabilities and functionality more broadly (as opposed to thinking, *This bit of tech works with M&A*). In addition, being an innovation lead can be lonely, and we wanted to avoid isolated people scattered around the firm, feeling as if they didn't belong to any team. We also wanted to be able to consolidate best practice and – as I have said many times – P&I (to which we include genAI) is very much a people sport. In my opinion, it's better for everyone in an innovation team to know a bit of everything, rather than stick to the only practice or process they know about. This is not to say that people in the innovation team cannot or do not have preferences, or develop more expertise in one area than another, but it is best for all members to have the same broad foundation as a knowledge base.

Although we have a centralized P&I department, the PIP roles ensure we receive wider firm and client insight. Each PIP is aligned to one of our client-facing segments. They spend 60 percent of their time on P&I, with their remaining time spent performing their previous day job, which could be legal work, managing client relationships, internal management, or a mixture of all three. This ensures that they retain their connection to the client and the legal work, allowing us to hear problems from and discuss ideas with clients directly. PIPs sit at the intersection between clients and business services; while they have some technological knowledge, they are not expected to code. Rather, their role is to understand the capabilities of the innovation tech stack in the broadest sense, to identify how they can be applied to solve client problems, and to share client problems, so that the rest of the P&I team can figure out potential solutions.

With the advent of genAI, we moved some of the innovation team into a new R&D team, with a focus on piloting emerging technologies, which meant that we did not dilute the wider innovation focus that others in the department had. The product, innovation, and R&D teams each have a respective manager who reports to me as the director of product and innovation. For us, it made sense to build innovation out into a wider department with sub-teams, because it allowed us to benefit from our track record. Although there is lots of work in relation to genAI in many firms, we took the view that our existing methodologies and ways of working for broader innovation – such as training and pilot processes; the skills developed around managing different stakeholders; and broader problem-solving abilities – fitted best alongside our innovation team. That isn't to say that the innovation team do not use genAI when it is the right solution to a particular problem – it exists, alongside many other things, as a useful option in the innovation toolkit. However, the department doesn't see it as the answer to everything, which allows the R&D team to trial different products, some of which never see the light of day. This also keeps genAI knowledge – particularly when looking to compare multiple similar products – deep and focused.

Culture and incentives: Integrating other specialists into partnership-led environments

My background as a lawyer has helped me enormously in my P&I roles in terms of understanding the legal domain, professional and operational constraints, and the client world. Conversely, my P&I roles have helped me enormously in securing promotions to fixed-share and then equity partnership, as they gave me the opportunity to expand beyond my day job: to develop my skills; solve wider business problems; build things clients wanted; and turn talk about innovation into something tangible. While not everyone aspires to partnership, in some firms, we see professionals without a legal background attaining partnership as a business services head, thereby fitting into the traditional law firm hierarchy, where both their rules and culture permit.

In short, for successful innovation, culture and incentives must reinforce each other and point in the same direction. A firm cannot say it wants innovation while:

- Rewarding only chargeable hours or income billed;
- Treating failed experiments as liabilities; or
- Expecting innovation to happen in fleeting moments of spare time.

As a sweeping generalization, lawyers are often cautious, skeptical, highly autonomous, and uncomfortable with not knowing the answer. These characteristics do not naturally align with being "innovative", but our experience shows that it is possible to create a culture that can actively support innovation. Innovation is a hearts and minds game, but culture should not just be a warm fuzzy feeling; it should be built and – more importantly – signaled through leadership and actions. Culture shows up in whether colleagues trust the process, collaborate well, are happy to provide ideas, work on new projects, or are willing to change how they work.

Strong board sponsorship has been vital to establishing an innovation culture at Weightmans. Active signals of this culture include:

- *Visible senior support:* This can include senior staff being vocal about pilots they have been involved in and actively encouraging others to join in; innovation being one of the update topics at firm-wide town hall meetings; hosting an innovation session on all leadership programs; an innovation element built into senior promotions; and public acknowledgment of those involved in successful projects on firm-wide recognition platforms.
- *Bringing together innovation teams, lawyers, and other experts to solve a problem:* No amount of internal comms about collaboration can send a stronger cultural signal than having board members and senior lawyers working together on a particular problem, with everyone bringing their disparate skills together to find a solution.
- *Failing fast, learning lessons, and going again:* If a failed innovation project leads to the team being disbanded, you may be in innovation theater territory!

It is vital that it is not just innovation leadership who are incentivized and "fit" from a cultural perspective. It is also critical for those working in product and leadership teams to see progression routes for themselves, in the same way that a newly qualified lawyer can see their pathway. At Weightmans, we have focused on providing the team with a wide variety of training in areas ranging from technical skills, stakeholder management, sales, LinkedIn, leadership, and everything inbetween. This has allowed us to expand and create promotion opportunities that those already in the team have been upskilled for, and we have seen people who began as junior members now running their own teams. It's particularly satisfying to be able to offer junior legal engineer roles that are genuinely entry-level, with no legal or innovation skills required, and watch these team members pick up a wide variety of new skills and flourish into legal engineer or senior legal engineer roles.

Incentivization is dependent upon the size and scale of your organization. You can be incredibly well-remunerated financially, but still have little impact culturally. Innovation in law firms is very much a people and leadership issue as much as it is a technology one: culture is a foundational enabler for innovation, while incentives make innovation worth doing. Warm words of support are not enough to sustain innovation in a law firm. Traditional incentives are often counterintuitive to innovation, with their focus on short-term revenue generation and billable hours. Often, the work involved on innovation projects is not chargeable and, therefore, easier to deprioritize. Recognizing innovation in a meaningful way and ensuring it is sustainable requires real organizational effort. This includes:

- *Time allocation:* This must be more than lip service and means actually freeing up the relevant experts when they are needed.
- *Budget:* This covers things like training and pilots and may include the licensing costs if a product is adopted. Without funds to experiment with, it is hard for innovation to gain traction, as there will always be other competing budget pressures.
- *Formal roles:* If innovation isn't someone's job, it is difficult for it to get done, as other roles and pressures will take priority. At Weightmans, we created full-time P&I roles and 60/40 split roles for PIPs in an effort to counter this. We have also established six-month trainee and apprentice seats within the department, to continue to upskill colleagues as they start their careers.
- *Visible leadership support:* See above.

Firms that normalize curiosity, lateral thinking, experimentation, and collaboration are usually those that can more successfully embed innovation.

The shift to organizing teams around "products"

So, how did we shift from an innovation team, situated within an existing law firm function, to a P&I department capable of "swarming" around ideas that we could turn into products and sell? As with most of our innovation journey, there was a fair amount of trial-and-error and some rather serendipitous luck!

Our journey began with a "gold dust lawyer" with an idea to turn his defense regulatory work in the transport arena into a proactive tool that clients could use to mitigate their operational risks. After approaching us for help, he spoke to his clients to outline the idea and to sense-check its viability. Buoyed by positive client feedback, the brilliant innovation team and a PIP translated the idea into a software prototype, Transport Manager Comply, which fulfilled the lawyer's expectations and was ready to show to his clients. The clients loved it, and we sold it. We could not believe our luck – if we, as a group of lawyers, could sell software to clients, imagine what we could do if professional product and sales skills were incorporated into the team! So, that's exactly what we did (Table 1).

Table 1. Case study: Transport Manager Comply

Challenge/ opportunity	Our early efforts on sales and preparation for conferences by a group of lawyers were not scalable or focused, and lacked the commercial edge that we knew our clients would expect. Client demos and discussions took priority over other existing work, and it was hard to ensure other innovation projects continued at the pace we wanted.
People	We recruited for a product manager and sales and demo roles to plug expertise gaps. Creation of the product manager role ensured overall ownership of all levels of the product lifecycle, from concept to retirement. Crucially, it was an opportunity to entwine our innovation and product processes and to focus on their prioritization and commercialization.

continued on next page

People *continued*	Our commercial manager and product specialist roles ensure that we have people who are thinking about clients and speaking with them about what matters to them. This includes keeping abreast of developments in both their industry and adjacent ones. This means that we are having conversations with clients that matter to them about their world. It also ensures that client demos are tailored to them, with the latest insight shared from the wider market. Our approach to conferences in terms of positioning and outreach has dramatically improved, with the team arriving at conferences with demos already pre-booked, as these tasks are now part of a product team's wider preparation. With our product team keeping close to clients, they can pick up new client requirements and act as the voice of the customer in our internal meetings. We have been able to develop the software at a pace and in ways we did not initially envisage. For example, when working with clients, we have built out data that they wanted. This, in turn, has helped our clients to leverage the software to secure new contracts and pitch for new business, particularly when competing against larger logistics firms. They have used it to profile their health and safety and compliance credentials, using data that our app captured, in their pitch documents. They have provided their prospective clients with evidence-based data that demonstrate their commitment to compliance and operational efficiency. These data points have been crucial in setting them apart by offering a distinct and competitive edge.
Process	Early in our innovation efforts, we created steering groups for each product to progress a wide variety

continued on next page

Process *continued*	of tasks and deal with any blockers. With the advent of a product team, we have been able to develop this into: • *Lead product role (commercial manager)*, responsible for governance and reporting. This is the person closest to the client need, who has their finger on the pulse of industry news and who has built strong relationships with the SMEs in the legal team. • *Project board*, which replaces steering group and becomes a very high-level bimonthly update of risks, issues, decisions, and blockers. • *Commercial delivery stream*, which is owned by the lead product role, with marketing and the product team involved for all sales and marketing activity. This replaces the need for specific sales and campaigns meetings and empowers the experts to deliver the campaigns while freeing up the agenda of the project board. • *Technical delivery stream*, which is owned by the innovation manger and supported by the lead product role, as the voice of the customer, and the lawyer SME, to approve legal changes. This is technical: tool changes, user account management, setting up bespoke apps, and so on.
What did we learn?	1. While initially useful to show viability, ad-hoc, lawyer-led sales activity is not scalable and lacks consistent commercial sharpness. Our changes resulted in more targeted, client-relevant demos and conference engagement with stronger commercial positioning better aligned to client expectations. 2. As products scale and develop, overly broad steering groups that are initially useful can create inefficiencies. Changing the governance structure by separating out commercial and technical delivery streams ensured greater focus, pace and clarity.

Challenges and lessons learned: Making multidisciplinary teams work

In multidisciplinary environments:

- Governance stops innovation becoming chaos;
- Ownership gives it momentum and stops it becoming someone else's problem;
- Adoption gives it a life beyond a pilot; and
- Managing resistance is what stops the whole thing being quietly stifled.

In my experience, multidisciplinary teams work best when they are genuinely mixed, mildly uncomfortable, and pointed at the same problem. Table 2 sets out some of the lessons I have learnt along the way.

Table 2. Lessons learned

Lesson learned	Why it works	Common pitfalls	Why it goes wrong
Curate for diversity of skills, rather than headcount	People with different backgrounds and expertise bring different ways of looking at, understanding, and solving a problem	Assembling a team that is too narrow or too similar	A team made up of people with the same training, background, or mindset is more likely to miss options, recycle familiar solutions, and stay trapped in one way of thinking
Cognitive diversity is more important than job titles	People who think differently challenge assumptions and avoid echo chambers. "Rebel ideas" and varied perspectives are productive, rather than disruptive	Groupthink or hierarchical thinking	Projects get skewed by consensus pressure, seniority, or comfort with the familiar, rather than being improved through constructive challenge and debate. You do not want projects to dutifully follow rank, rather than sense

continued on next page

Lesson learned	Why it works	Common pitfalls	Why it goes wrong
A degree of friction is healthy – there is no monopoly on the ability to have a good idea	It is no good having a multidisciplinary team on paper if everyone is too polite, too similar, or too seniority-conscious to challenge anything	The loudest voice wins	If everything gets bent around the most senior, forceful or convinced person in the room, the rest of the team may as well not be there
The right people need to be in the same room at the right time	The room needs to include the people who understand the client problem, the operational reality, and the available technical capability. The room needs to hear this firsthand and be able to ask the questions they need to	Wrong room composition misses important perspectives	You end up solving the wrong problem, designing something unworkable, or discovering late in the day that key operational, technical, or user constraints were missed or misinterpreted
Balance thinkers, planners, and doers	A blend of big-picture thinkers, planners, practical doers, and detail-focused people enhances creativity and execution discipline	Too much of one type	Too much thinking, and you risk drifting into inertia. Too many doers, and you race ahead without enough structure or reflection

continued on next page

Lesson learned	Why it works	Common pitfalls	Why it goes wrong
Make it safe to experiment across different disciplines	Psychological safety ensures iterative experimentation and makes it safe for people to have a go. Multidisciplinary teams work when people are comfortable testing ideas, sharing half-formed or imperfect thinking, and learning from what does not work, rather than feeling silly or defensive	Low trust and fear of failure	Innovation is choked when people feel they will be blamed, contradicted, or embarrassed; they contribute and challenge less and avoid risk. At that point, you no longer have a collaborative team; you have adjacent professionals politely disappointing each other
You cannot overcommunicate	Repeated communication, shared messaging, and visible explanations of what the team is doing, why it matters, and how people can engage are key to building a sense of belonging and shared success. Keep talking, even when you think everyone understands. Different disciplines use different shorthand, have different	Assuming alignment will magically happen	Different disciplines work with different assumptions and vocabularies. Without active and frequent communication, misunderstanding and drift can set in quickly. Do not assume is aligned because they were in the meeting. They often are not. People leave with entirely different understandings of what was agreed, what matters most, and what happens next

continued on next page

Lesson learned	Why it works	Common pitfalls	Why it goes wrong
You cannot overcommunicate *continued*	assumptions, and different definitions of success. You must keep translating, repeating, and checking that everyone is still talking about the same thing		
Multidisciplinary thinking needs to be combined with process discipline and governance, even if the governance gets refined	Successful multidisciplinary work is not random brainstorming. Teams still need clear objectives, problem statements, priorities, owners, pilot discipline, governance, and feedback loops Governance gives people clarity on decision-making, accountability, risk management, and how work moves from idea to delivery, rather than relying on goodwill and crossed fingers	Mistaking collaboration for unstructured (faster) chaos and limited structure because everyone is trying to be "agile"	Teams can take on too much, prioritize poorly, and struggle to scale, especially as demand grows Do not mistake energy for progress. A room full of clever people, sharpies, and Post-It notes can feel productive but, if there is no method behind it, you just end up with a lot of enthusiasm and not much achieved It goes wrong when decisions are implied, rather than made, and everyone slowly discovers that nobody is entirely sure who approved what, when, or why

continued on next page

Lesson learned	Why it works	Common pitfalls	Why it goes wrong
Ownership needs to be clearly allocated, but innovation cannot be treated as the responsibility of one team alone	Clear ownership creates accountability and momentum. Shared involvement keeps lawyers, business services, and innovation teams invested in the outcome, rather than watching from a safe distance	Innovation gets dumped on one team and admired from afar (ie, "We have told them our brilliant idea so need to have no more involvement")	It goes wrong when the innovation team is expected to speak to the client, produce the idea, know the legal framework, build it, land it, secure adoption, and prove the value, while everyone else remains on the periphery and retains the belief that none of this is really their problem
Resistance from others should be expected and managed deliberately, rather than treated as an inconvenient surprise	Resistance is something that can be understood and worked with through early engagement, realistic expectations, practical training, and honest communication	The team assumes that the logic of the solution will be enough to win people over	It goes wrong when users are rolled over by a solution that is supposedly self-evidently brilliant, only for them to ignore it, resist it, criticize it, or simply wait for the whole thing to pass

References

1 Whittle S and Wolfenden C, *Innovation in Law Firms: Implementing Successful Projects*, Globe Law and Business; 2024.

2 *Ibid.*

Chapter 8:
From roles to systems: How AI is reshaping legal decision infrastructure

By Olga V. Mack, CEO, TermScout

The misdiagnosis

Consider a typical contract negotiation. Weeks of redlines go back and forth; each side asserts that its position is "market", but neither has clear visibility into what that actually means. Decisions are driven by experience, instinct, or precedent, and outcomes vary widely depending on who is negotiating and how much leverage they have. Now consider an eDiscovery protocol: counsel meet and confer over the scope, custodians, and search terms; positions shift from matter to matter: and similar issues are argued repeatedly without a consistent baseline. Costs expand, scope creeps, and disputes resurface in slightly different forms each time. These do not look like the same problem, but they are.

Most conversations about artificial intelligence (AI) in law focus on new roles: legal engineers; data scientists; and AI governance leads. The assumption is that the transformation of legal work will be defined by who does the work, but this is the wrong place to direct our focus. What is actually changing is more fundamental than that. Legal is shifting from document-centric work to system-driven decision-making. The focus is moving away from drafting and reviewing individual documents toward structuring how decisions are made, executed, and monitored over time.

Contracts and electronically stored information (ESI) protocols sit at the center of this shift. They are often treated as static outputs: documents to be negotiated, filed, and stored. In practice, they do much more. They allocate risk, define acceptable behavior, and shape how parties act over time. They are not endpoints; they are mechanisms. Seen this way, contracts and ESI protocols are not documents. They are decision systems: they take inputs, translate them into structured positions, guide execution, and require ongoing monitoring to ensure alignment with expectations.

Once legal work is understood as a set of decision systems, the emergence of new roles becomes easier to explain. These roles are not arbitrary additions, but are instead responses to gaps in the design, implementation, and governance of those systems. If you understand the system, the roles make sense. If you do not, the roles look fragmented.

Core framework: The Legal Decision Stack

To understand what is changing in legal work, it helps to move from thinking in terms of documents to thinking in terms of systems. The Legal Decision Stack provides a simple way to do that. It breaks legal work into a set of layers that together define how decisions are made, executed, and monitored over time. At a high level, the stack consists of five layers:

1. Layer 1: Inputs;
2. Layer 2: Translation;
3. Layer 3: Decision logic;
4. Layer 4: Execution; and
5. Layer 5: Monitoring.

Before defining each layer in detail, consider a familiar example. In a contract negotiation, the inputs include the draft agreement, prior templates, internal policies, and the counterparty's proposed terms. These inputs are not directly actionable; they must be structured. That structured understanding informs decisions about what to accept, reject, or escalate. Those decisions are then executed through negotiation and drafting. After signature, the contract continues to shape behavior and must be monitored over time for compliance, renewal, and drift from expectations.

The same structure applies in eDiscovery. Rules, standing orders, and prior protocols form the inputs. These are translated into structured requirements and defensible positions. Those positions inform decisions about scope, proportionality, and burden. Decisions are executed through meet-and-confer discussions and drafted protocols. Over time, compliance, cost, and scope must be monitored. Across both domains, the system is the same.

Inputs

The first layer consists of the raw materials of legal work: contracts, policies, rules, data, and prior work product. At this stage, information is largely unstructured. It exists as text, precedent, or institutional knowledge. Lawyers, knowledge management (KM) professionals, and data teams play a central role here, gathering and maintaining the information that feeds the system.

Translation

The second layer converts inputs into something usable. Clauses are classified, provisions are compared, and requirements are structured. In contracts, this may involve benchmarking terms against a broader dataset. In eDiscovery, it may involve translating rules and orders into concrete obligations. This is where legal engineers and data scientists are most active, building the structures that enable consistent comparison and analysis of information.

Decision logic

The third layer defines how choices are made. This includes rules, thresholds, escalation paths, and risk tolerances. For example, which deviations from the market are acceptable? When should a position be escalated? What constitutes a defensible scope in discovery? Senior lawyers, risk functions, and AI governance roles are central here, setting the parameters that guide decisions across matters.

Execution

The fourth layer is where decisions are put into action. In contracts, this includes negotiation, drafting, and approval workflows. In eDiscovery, it includes meet-and-confer discussions, protocol drafting, and court submissions. Lawyers remain deeply involved at this layer, supported by legal operations and, increasingly, systems that automate or assist parts of the workflow.

Monitoring

The fifth layer extends the system beyond the initial decision. Contracts must be tracked for compliance, renewal, and performance against expectations. Discovery processes must be monitored for cost, scope, and adherence to agreed protocols. Legal operations, data teams, and AI governance functions play a key role in ensuring that decisions made at one point in time remain valid as circumstances evolve.

Decision flow: Inputs → Monitoring

Inputs
Contracts, policies, rules, data
Roles: Lawyers · KM · Data

Translation
Structuring into signals and patterns
Roles: Legal engineers · Data scientists

Decision Logic
Rules, thresholds, escalation
Roles: Senior lawyers · AI governance

Execution
Actions taken (human or system)
Roles: Lawyers · Legal ops

Monitoring
Drift, performance, feedback loops
Roles: Legal ops · Data · AI governance

Figure 1: Legal Decision Stack

Viewed together, these layers form a continuous system with a feedback loop. Decisions are not isolated events tied to individual documents; they are part of an ongoing cycle that begins with inputs, continues through monitoring, and feeds back into the next set of inputs.

This perspective also clarifies the role of emerging legal functions. Roles do not operate independently, but operate across layers of a system. Legal engineers do not simply "support" lawyers; they enable translation. Data teams do not only provide reporting; they support both translation and monitoring. AI governance is not an abstract function; it sits directly within decision logic and oversight. This is where roles emerge as owners of different parts of the decision lifecycle.

Once legal work is understood in this way, the proliferation of new roles is no longer surprising. It is a structural response to the need to design, operate, and govern decision systems that extend beyond any single document or moment.

Supporting framework: Signal vs. document

If the Legal Decision Stack explains how decisions are made, the shift from documents to signals explains what those decisions are made from. Legal work has traditionally been organized around documents. Contracts, policies, pleadings, and protocols are treated as the primary unit of analysis. They are drafted, reviewed, negotiated, and stored. Each document is largely evaluated on its own terms, often with limited visibility into how it compares to others. Documents, by their nature, are static: they capture a position at a given moment. They are also difficult to compare at scale, especially when language varies across agreements or matters. As a result, decision-making is often fragmented and reactive, driven by individual experience rather than consistent, structured insight.

The shift is from documents to signals. Signals are structured representations of the contents of documents. They are measurable, comparable, and trackable over time. Instead of focusing on the document as a whole, signals extract and standardize the elements that matter for decision-making.

This becomes clearer with examples. In contracts, a clause is not yet a signal. It is text. Once that clause is classified, benchmarked, and compared across a portfolio or market dataset, it becomes a signal. That signal can then be aggregated into patterns – for example, how often a particular risk allocation appears; how far a given position deviates from market norms; or how a company's agreements cluster over time. Those patterns inform decisions: whether to accept, push back, or escalate a given term. In practice, this can reveal that a significant portion of agreements deviate from market norms in ways that are not visible when reviewing contracts individually.

Clause → signal → portfolio pattern → decision

In eDiscovery, a rule or standing order is, at the outset, just text. It becomes useful when translated into structured requirements: what must be produced, within what scope, and under what constraints. Across matters and judges, those requirements can be compared to identify patterns in how discovery is approached and enforced. Those patterns become signals that inform strategy: how to position arguments, where to expect resistance, and how to manage scope and cost.

Rule → requirement → pattern across judges → strategy signal

Across both domains, the transformation is identical: text is converted into structured inputs that can be analyzed, compared, and used to guide decisions over time. The role of AI in this shift is often misunderstood. AI does not make documents valuable; documents have always contained valuable information. AI enables the consistent extraction, classification, and structuring of that information into usable signals. Without that structure, more documents simply mean more text to review. With it, they become a source of insight.

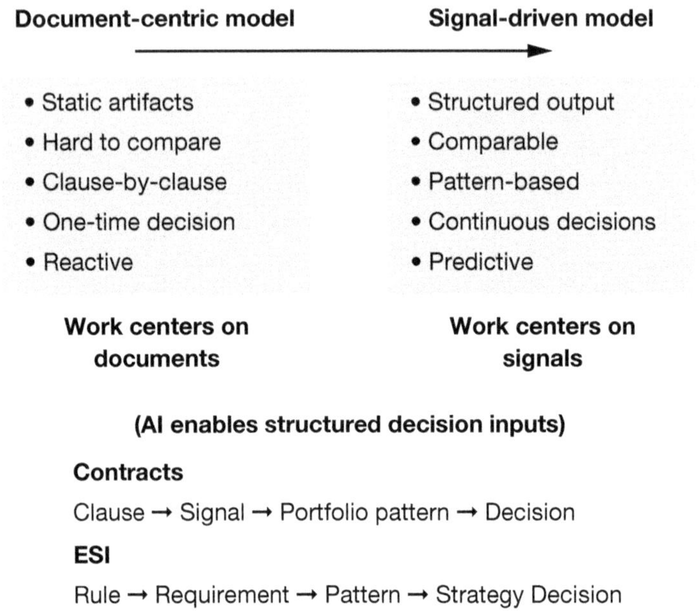

Figure 2: From documents to signals

This shift also clarifies the role of emerging functions within legal organizations. Data teams, legal engineers, and KM professionals are not operating at the margins. They are central to converting unstructured text into usable inputs for decision-making. They define taxonomies, build models, maintain datasets, and ensure that signals are accurate, consistent, and meaningful.

Once signals are in place, decision-making changes materially. It becomes less about interpreting individual documents in isolation and more about understanding patterns, deviations, and trends. This allows legal teams to move from reactive responses to more consistent, informed, and ultimately predictive decision-making.

The move from documents to signals is not a change in format; it is a change in how legal work is understood and performed.

Supporting framework: The Risk-Tiered Action Model

If the Legal Decision Stack explains how decisions are structured, and the shift from documents to signals explains what decisions are made from, the Risk-Tiered Action Model explains how those decisions translate into action.

Not all actions in legal workflows carry the same level of risk. Some are purely informational; others result in binding commitments with legal and financial consequences. Treating all actions as equivalent creates either over-control or under-governance. A more useful approach is to distinguish actions by tier.

The model consists of four tiers:

1. Tier 1: Informational;
2. Tier 2: Recommendation;
3. Tier 3: Internal action; and
4. Tier 4: External commitment.

Tier 1: Informational

At Tier 1, the system provides analysis without suggesting or taking action. This includes summarization, extraction, and classification – for example, identifying key clauses in a contract or summarizing discovery obligations under a court order. The output informs human judgment but does not guide it. Risk at this level is relatively low, as no decisions are being made or acted upon.

Tier 2: Recommendation

At Tier 2, the system suggests possible actions. In contracts, this might include proposed redlines or flags indicating deviations from market norms. In eDiscovery, it may involve suggested positions on scope or proportionality. The system influences decisions, but humans retain control. Risk increases, as recommendations can shape outcomes, but oversight remains straightforward.

Tier 3: Internal action

At Tier 3, decisions are executed within the organization – for example, a narrow category of low-risk agreements can be auto-approved within predefined thresholds. This includes approvals, automated routing, or system-driven changes to workflows. At this level, actions have operational impact, even if they do not yet bind external parties. Risk is higher, and governance must ensure that decision logic is sound and consistently applied.

Tier 4: External commitment

At Tier 4, actions result in binding positions. This includes signing contracts, commitment to negotiated terms, or submission of discovery protocols to a court. At this level, decisions carry legal and financial consequences. Errors are costly. Oversight must be rigorous. Human judgment, accountability, and clear governance structures are critical.

These tiers can be illustrated through familiar workflows.

In contracts:
Analysis → suggested redline → approval → signing
In eDiscovery:
Summary → proposed position → drafted protocol → court commitment

Across both examples, the progression is consistent: information becomes a recommendation; a recommendation becomes an action; and an action becomes a commitment.

The key point is straightforward: the higher the tier, the more that governance is required. Informational outputs can be scaled with relatively light oversight. Recommendations require validation and review. Internal actions require defined controls and auditability. External commitments require clear ownership, accountability, and often human approval.

This structure also clarifies how roles align with risk. Lower tiers are typically supported by data, engineering, and knowledge functions. These roles focus on extracting, structuring, and presenting information in a consistent, reliable manner. Their work enables scale but does not, on its own, determine outcomes. Higher tiers are dominated by legal, risk, and governance roles. These functions are responsible for setting thresholds, approving actions, and ensuring that decisions align with organizational objectives and legal obligations. They carry accountability for outcomes, particularly where external commitments are involved.

Seen together, the tiers provide a practical way to think about how AI and systems should be deployed within legal workflows. The question is not whether to use technology, but at which tier, and under what level of control. By aligning actions with risk, legal teams can scale lower-risk activities while preserving appropriate oversight where it matters most.

Higher risk and impact ↑

Tier 4: External Commitment
Legal/financial impact
Examples: Signing, court positions
Roles: Senior lawyers · Governance

Tier 3: Internal Action
System/workflow changes
Examples: Approvals, automation
Roles: Legal ops · Systems

Tier 2: Recommendation
Suggested actions
Examples: Redlines, strategy
Roles: Legal engineers · AI

Tier 1: Informational analysis only
Examples: Summaries, extraction
Roles: Data · KM

Lower risk and impact

Figure 3: Risk-Tiered Action Model

Example 1: Contracts as decision systems

Contracts are treated as static agreements. They are negotiated, signed, and stored. However, in practice, they function as ongoing decision systems that shape vendor behavior over time. Viewed through the Legal Decision Stack, the structure is clear.

At the Inputs layer, contracts begin as text. This includes draft agreements, standard templates, fallback language, and historical contracts. Clauses are the raw material. They contain the substance of risk allocation, obligations, and commercial terms, but in an unstructured form. Lawyers, KM, and data teams maintain and curate these inputs, ensuring that prior work and institutional knowledge are accessible.

At the Translation layer, those inputs are converted into structured signals. Clauses are classified; provisions are normalized; and terms are benchmarked against a broader dataset. This is where a contract becomes insight.

Without this layer, decisions remain dependent on individual judgment rather than consistent benchmarks. For example, a limitation of liability clause is not only read, but positioned relative to market norms. A termination provision is not only interpreted but compared across a portfolio. Legal engineers and data teams play a central role here, building the systems that make this translation consistent and scalable.

At the Decision logic layer, structured signals inform choices. The question is no longer simply "What does this clause say?" but, "Is this acceptable? Does it deviate from market? Should it be escalated?" Decision logic defines thresholds: which terms can be accepted, which require negotiation, and which must be escalated. Senior lawyers, risk functions, and governance roles set and refine these parameters, ensuring that decisions align with the organization's risk tolerance and commercial objectives.

At the Execution layer, decisions are acted upon. This is where negotiation occurs: redlines are proposed; positions are adjusted; and agreements are finalized. Execution is increasingly supported by systems that guide workflows, suggest language, and automate low-risk approvals. Lawyers remain central, but legal operations and systems are playing an increasingly important role in ensuring consistent, efficient execution.

At the Monitoring layer, the system continues after the signature. Contracts are not the end; they define obligations that must be tracked over time. Renewal dates, performance obligations, and risk positions must be monitored to ensure that the agreement continues to align with expectations. Drift can occur, as market standards evolve or as vendor behavior diverges from contractual terms. Legal operations and data teams are essential here, maintaining visibility into how agreements perform across the portfolio.

This structure maps directly to the design of contract intelligence platforms:

- At the point of execution, deals are managed in flight. This is where negotiation decisions are made, supported by signals and benchmarks.
- At the monitoring stage, agreements are tracked post-signature. The focus shifts from closing the deal to ensuring that the contract continues to perform as intended.
- At the portfolio level, patterns emerge. This is often where hidden concentrations of risk become visible for the first time. Aggregated signals reveal concentrations of risk, recurring deviations, and systemic issues across vendors and agreements.

- At the market level, an external baseline provides context. Organizations can see how their positions compare to broader norms, identifying where they are aligned or out of step.

These layers are not separate products; they are different perspectives on the same decision system. The key point is that contracts govern behavior over time – not only at the moment of signing. They influence how vendors perform, how risk is allocated, and how disputes are managed. Without a system to translate, execute, and monitor those decisions, contracts remain static documents. With it, they become a mechanism for ongoing governance.

Different roles support each layer of this system in practice. Lawyers interpret and negotiate. Legal engineers and data teams structure and benchmark. Legal operations ensure consistency and visibility across workflows. Governance functions define thresholds and oversee outcomes. Together, they operate not around documents, but across a system that continuously shapes decisions.

Example 2: ESI protocols as decision systems

ESI protocols are treated as procedural documents tied to a single matter. They are negotiated, filed, and then largely set aside unless disputes arise. In practice, they function as decision systems that shape how discovery is conducted over the life of a case and, increasingly, across matters. Viewed through the same Legal Decision Stack, the structure is consistent with contracts, despite the fact that the context is different.

At the Inputs layer, the raw materials include federal rules, local rules, judge-specific standing orders, prior protocols, and the facts of the case. These inputs define what is permissible, expected, and contested in discovery. Like contracts, they are unstructured at the outset. Lawyers rely on experience and prior work but, without a consistent system, similar issues are approached differently across matters. This leads to repeated arguments and inconsistent outcomes across cases with similar facts.

At the Translation layer, those inputs are converted into structured requirements. Rules and orders are interpreted and distilled into actionable obligations: which data must be collected; how these should be processed; what formats are required; and what limits may apply. Prior protocols can be analyzed to identify common positions or acceptable ranges. This translation creates a usable decision framework, instead of an ad-hoc interpretation.

Legal engineers, KM, and data-oriented roles are critical here, ensuring that requirements are consistently defined and reusable.

At the Decision logic layer, structured requirements inform choices about scope and proportionality. What custodians should be included? What date ranges are defensible? What search terms are appropriate? These decisions are not made in isolation; they are shaped by risk tolerance, cost considerations, and judicial expectations. Decision logic defines when to narrow the scope, when to push back, and when to escalate. Senior lawyers and litigation strategists lead here, supported by governance functions that aim to ensure consistency and defensibility across matters.

At the Execution layer, decisions are translated into action. This includes meet-and-confer discussions, drafting of ESI protocols, and, where necessary, motion practice. Positions are articulated, negotiated, and formalized. As with contracts, execution is not purely manual. Structured inputs and prior positions can inform drafting, guide negotiation, and reduce variability. Lawyers remain central, but workflows and supporting systems increasingly shape how consistently those decisions are applied.

At the Monitoring layer, the system continues beyond the initial agreement. Discovery is not static: scope can expand; costs can increase; and disputes can arise as new information emerges. Monitoring involves tracking protocol compliance, managing production volumes, and identifying when the scope or cost deviates from expectations. Without visibility, discovery can drift significantly from what was initially agreed. Legal operations and data functions are essential here, providing the insight needed to manage ongoing obligations and adjust strategy as needed.

Across all layers, the pattern is consistent: inputs are structured; decisions are made; actions are taken; and outcomes are monitored. The key point is that litigation, particularly in the context of eDiscovery, is not a one-time advocacy exercise, but an ongoing managed system. It is managed through structured decision systems that operate over time. Each decision about scope, burden, and proportionality feeds into a broader system that determines cost, risk, and defensibility.

This perspective also clarifies the role of emerging functions within litigation teams. Roles emerge to manage consistency, defensibility, and monitoring across matters. KM ensures that prior positions and protocols are accessible and reusable. Data and technical specialists structure requirements and track outcomes. Legal operations support workflow and visibility. Senior lawyers define strategy and make judgment calls at critical points.

When these roles operate within a defined system, outcomes become more consistent and defensible. When they do not, similar issues are resolved differently across cases, increasing both risk and cost.

Seen alongside contracts, ESI protocols reinforce the same underlying shift. Different domains, different documents, but the same structure: legal work organized as a system of decisions rather than a collection of isolated artifacts.

Why roles are emerging

The discussion of contracts and ESI protocols points back to a broader theme: the rise of new roles is not the primary transformation; instead, it is the visible result of a deeper structural shift. Roles exist because systems need owners, and each layer of the system requires a different type of expertise and accountability. As legal work moves from document-centric tasks to system-driven decision-making, each layer of the Legal Decision Stack requires dedicated expertise. Where those capabilities did not exist, new roles emerged to fill the gap.

At the Inputs layer, KM plays a central role. This function is responsible for curating templates, prior work product, and institutional knowledge. Without structured inputs, downstream decision-making becomes inconsistent and inefficient. KM is not simply about storage; it is about ensuring that the right information is available in a usable form.

At the Translation layer, legal engineers and data specialists convert unstructured text into structured signals. This includes building taxonomies, classifying clauses, and creating systems that allow for comparison across agreements and matters. Legal engineers bridge legal expertise and technical implementation, enabling the consistent transformation of documents into usable data.

Closely related is the Signal layer, where data scientists and analytics functions operate. Their role is to aggregate, analyze, and surface patterns across portfolios and datasets. This is where individual data points become insights, and where organizations gain visibility into trends, deviations, and risk concentrations.

At the Decision logic layer, AI governance and senior legal roles define how decisions are made. This includes setting thresholds, defining escalation paths, and ensuring that automated or assisted decisions align with legal and organizational standards. Governance functions are responsible for maintaining accountability as systems scale.

At the Execution and Monitoring layers, legal operations play a critical role. Execution requires consistent workflows, coordination across stakeholders, and, increasingly, integration with systems that guide or automate parts of the process. Monitoring extends that responsibility over time, ensuring that decisions remain valid, obligations are met, and deviations are identified and addressed.

Across these layers, the pattern is consistent. Each role corresponds to a specific function within the decision system. No role operates in isolation: each depends on the others to maintain coherence across the lifecycle of decisions.

The key point is that firms are not adding roles randomly; instead, they are filling gaps in the decision stack. When legal work was centered on individual documents, many of these functions were implicit, distributed, or handled informally by lawyers themselves. As systems become more complex and scalable, those responsibilities require dedicated ownership. The emergence of new roles reflects the need for clarity, consistency, and control across an increasingly scalable system. Seen this way, the proliferation of roles is not fragmentation – it is a specialization aligned to structure.

Implications for leadership

The shift from documents to decision systems changes how legal organizations are led and structured. It requires a different way of thinking about work, performance, and ownership. First, leaders should stop organizing around document types. Structuring teams around contracts, litigation, or compliance reflects a document-centric view of legal work. While these categories remain relevant, they do not capture how decisions are actually made. The same underlying system applies across domains. Organizing around decision systems, instead of document categories, creates alignment across functions that would otherwise operate in silos.

Second, leaders should start organizing around decision systems. This requires identifying the core decision flows within the organization and mapping how they move from inputs through execution and monitoring. It also means recognizing where those systems are incomplete or inconsistent. Once visible, they can be designed, improved, and scaled deliberately.

Third, leaders should measure signal quality, not output volume. Traditional metrics often focus on the number of contracts reviewed; the number of documents processed; or the speed at which work is completed. These measure activity, not effectiveness. In a system-driven model, the more relevant question is whether decisions are consistent, defensible, and aligned with market or organizational standards. Signal quality, accuracy, and the usefulness of structured inputs become more meaningful indicators of performance. It reflects whether the system is producing reliable, comparable, and actionable inputs.

Fourth, leaders should define ownership across the stack. Each layer of the Legal Decision Stack requires clear accountability. Who is responsible for maintaining inputs? Who ensures that translation is accurate and consistent? Who defines decision logic? Who oversees execution and monitors outcomes? Without clear ownership, systems fragment and revert to ad-hoc decision-making. With it, organizations can scale without losing control.

These shifts do not require abandoning existing structures. They require reframing them. Legal teams can continue to support contracts, litigation, and compliance while also operating across shared decision systems that bring consistency and visibility. Legal is not adding roles. It is becoming the function that defines how decisions are made, executed, and monitored across the business.

Chapter 9:
The AI-enabled professional: Skills, culture, and adoption in the modern law firm

By Paul Caddy, managing knowledge lawyer, Lewis Silkin LLP

"Look, Matty, I'm computing!"[1] says a young Jennifer Aniston to fellow *Friends* star Matthew Perry. The duo are starring in "the world's first cyber-sitcom"[2] to show viewers how to use a newly launched operating system. At the launch event, a 39-year-old CEO dances on stage in front of thousands of excited techies. The Rolling Stones' 1981 hit *Start Me Up* blasts out of TV sets across the world. In total, $300 million has reportedly been spent on the launch campaign.[3] Have you guessed the year and event yet?

It is 1995, and Microsoft has launched Windows 95. Thanks to this software, it is also the year that the Internet starts to enter the mainstream. "The Internet is a tidal wave. It changes the rules,"[4] Bill Gates noted in an internal memo about four months earlier. The world was changing, and Gates knew what was about to hit it.

More than 30 years later, we are in a similar place with generative AI (genAI), another game-changing technology that is upending ways of working, albeit in a fundamentally more disruptive way. OpenAI's ChatGPT was one of the fastest-growing internet applications ever, reaching 100 million users just two months after launch.[5] In December 2025, Microsoft CEO Satya Nadella said that the world is "entering a phase of widespread diffusion", but the vital and difficult questions of "how to shape its impact on the world"[6] have arisen.

Just as law firms grappled with Windows 95 and the internet in the mid-90s, lawyers need to prepare their businesses for AI now. This chapter focuses on the capabilities required for the emerging roles set out in the other chapters, including:

- The skills required for AI-enabled roles;
- The cultural and behavioral factors that drive the successful adoption of AI;
- The challenges of embedding new AI-powered tools into real workflows; and
- How to approach training and capability development.

Looking back at Windows 95, it is remarkable what users had to learn (even how to right-click!) and how quickly technologies were adopted. If you thought 1995 was transformational, the late 2020s will be seismic.

A note before we move on: this chapter concentrates on genAI, a subset of AI, which has seen rapid adoption in recent years. Many firms, however, have been using other AI, such as machine learning AI (in platforms like Kira and Luminance) for considerably longer. GenAI is the latest in a series of waves of AI development. So, let us begin with the first of these themes: the skills that lawyers and allied professionals need to work effectively with AI.

The skills required for AI-enabled roles

AI has the potential to be the most disruptive transformation since humans developed the capacity for abstract thought, many tens of thousands of years ago. The skills required for this intelligence revolution are novel, cross-disciplinary, and constantly evolving. Training in AI cannot be a standard tick-box exercise; this is not an area where you score 80 percent on ten multiple-choice questions and are deemed "good to go". While this technology is not without its faults, it is – in the words of Sir Geoffrey Vos, Master of the Rolls – "changing the way things are done in every conceivable sector of the global economy",[7] including the legal sector.

AI is transforming our world now. In a survey published in 2025 by KPMG, 71 percent of UK CEOs said that they are redesigning roles and career paths for AI collaboration.[8] Training on AI is vital, both for these redesigned jobs and for existing ones too. However, many key skills are lacking: the author's firm, Lewis Silkin, in its *Future @ Work* report, found that 44 percent of respondents to a global survey of 663 senior decision-makers say there is a shortage of AI literacy generally across the workforce.[9] In 2025, the AI Workforce Consortium noted that "high-severity gaps" in skills have emerged in areas as basic as competencies in large language models (LLMs), genAI, and prompt engineering. These gaps extend to AI ethics and security, too, which – as the Consortium notes – "jeopardize organizations' ability to scale AI responsibly, securely, and effectively".[10]

Firms should also ensure that they do not just focus training on how specific AI tools work, such as Legora or Harvey. Lawyers and non-lawyers (allied professionals) need a broader understanding of AI, as set out below.

General skills

Before we look at specific skills, there are general skills – and three key "meta-skills" – which people need to enable them to thrive in an age of AI. The first "meta-skill", which cuts across all those set out below, is an obvious one, but no less important for that: curiosity. When Michael Dell, chairman and CEO of Dell, was asked what attribute was most needed for success in turbulent times, he said: "I would place my bet on curiosity."[11] At a time of accelerated change, this often-overlooked skill is vital. It puts fire in the bellies of your people to be excited by AI (however, see this chapter's discussion on fighting the fear below).

The second meta-skill is the ability to pivot when circumstances change. After all, change is not the exception to the rule – it *is* the rule. People need to be comfortable with dealing with change, including in the skills that they need and the habits that they need to forgo. What follows is a baseline suite of skills, so that your people can use AI with confidence, spotting risks and seizing opportunities. They can broadly be grouped into technical understanding; legal and regulatory understanding; and knowing when and how to deploy AI responsibly. Firms need to revisit them regularly and reskill accordingly.

The third meta-skill – and perhaps the most important of the three – is critical thinking. This is the ability to question outputs from the technology that we use, such as AI, and not to accept them without any further thought.

Case study: Why critical thinking matters

In a world of increasing technological power, critical thinking is more important than ever. Take Stanislav Petrov, a lieutenant colonel in the Soviet Air Defense Forces. It is 1983, and he is sitting in front of his computer when he receives a warning that there is a nuclear missile strike incoming from the US. "All I had to do was to reach for the phone to raise the direct line to our top commanders,"[12] Petrov told the BBC 30 years later, but he started to suspect something was awry.

Petrov's suspicion – that it was a false alarm – is credited with saving the world from nuclear Armageddon. It was luck that he was the duty officer that morning. His colleagues were professional soldiers "taught to give and obey orders",[13] whereas he was the only one with a civilian education. His view? They would have picked up the phone unthinkingly. A retaliatory strike would have been launched.

Put simply, Petrov was taught how to think. Similarly, our people need to be experts in critical thinking. It is a skill that needs honing throughout a legal career. We are at a critical juncture: a senior university lecturer in a LexisNexis report, *The mentorship gap*, stated that, for lawyers in training, their experience was that there was "no critical reasoning, no belief in themselves and no confidence".[14]

The spike in AI use has also brought "cognitive offloading" to the fore – where users outsource much or all their thinking to AI and risk core skills declining.[15] This can result in "cognitive atrophy": "use it or lose it", so to speak. However, some research suggests that the key is to use AI mindfully: treat it as a "thought partner" and not "thought leader"; follow the rule of "think first, prompt second";[16] and know how to challenge and edit AI outputs. These skills are vital for lawyers to work alongside AI.

Understanding how AI works and what it can do

What is intelligence? There is no universal definition of it, and the same applies to artificial intelligence. However, this lack of consensus does not mean that you cannot train your people on AI. Failing to do so risks them thinking AI is akin to magic.

Not everyone who uses AI in a firm needs a BSc in applied computer science to use it, but they do need to understand the very basics of how it works. The focus will typically be on genAI, although, if the firm uses other types of AI, training should be provided on those too. Training typically includes:

- *What AI is:* Perhaps exploring some of the most common definitions – the UK Jurisdictional Taskforce defines it simply as "a technology that is autonomous".[17]
- *What LLMs are:* Perhaps using examples of hallucinated case citations as simply being predicted text patterns – this helps people understand why hallucinations happen (see the discussion of hallucinations and misgroundings below) and why LLMs are not intelligent in the way that humans think of intelligence.
- *What foundation models and frontier models are:* Examples could include OpenAI's GPT and Anthropic's Claude.
- *What agentic AI is (and AI agents are):* This is only if applicable.

Others may need more specialized training, depending on how technical their roles are.

Other skills include an understanding of:

- *The sycophantic nature of much AI:* Some models just want to be your virtual friend and will answer questions despite being unsure about

their answers (which is why some firms use prompts that ask their models not to present unverified or uncertain information as fact).
- *AI's tendency to hallucinate and "misground".*
- *The biases that affect AI:* These can embed and amplify the biases of their creators and the data on which it is trained.
- *AI's lack of transparency:* AI has a "black box" problem, where it is often impossible to understand why it has arrived at a particular output.
- *Other risks:* For more insight on these, the Massachusetts Institute of Technology (MIT) has created its AI Risk Navigator which is a useful tool to allow firms to "explore the full landscape of AI risk in one place".[18]

Other organizations have published useful materials to understand genAI generally, including Stanford University's 2026 *AI Index Annual Report 2026*.[19]

Understanding how we interact best with AI

People are creatures of habit, and understanding which habits will continue to serve us and which ones need to be jettisoned is key to firms getting the best out of AI. The author spoke to Roch Glowacki, partner at Lewis Silkin, who notes that lawyers are biased towards their existing workflows and habits. This could be, for example, preferring to use a keyboard as opposed to speaking to a computer, or a particular way of delegating tasks. Put simply, how we work now is not necessarily the most effective way to work with AI in the future.

Glowacki also says that many lawyers need to reconceptualize how they see AI. They often default to treating AI as if it is an eager virtual trainee solicitor;[20] however, lawyers can ask much more of AI, such as: "Give me a step-by-step detailed plan for solving this problem" or "Give me ten alternative ways to draft this clause". On a more fundamental level, lawyers need to "rethink their relationship with AI" to take full advantage of it. Firms' training should cover this dynamic thoughtfully and highlight the new ways of thinking that AI can engender, opening up exciting new opportunities to service client needs.

Understanding the current state of AI

What about the current state of AI? This is not unlike playing darts with a moving board. As the *2026 AI Index Annual Report* notes, the AI field "is scaling faster than the systems around it can adapt".[21]

It is helpful to train people on where AI is heading, answering questions such as: what is artificial narrow intelligence (ANI or "weak AI")? What is artificial general intelligence (AGI or "strong AI")? What is artificial superintelligence (ASI)? And what does this all mean in practice?

It is often said in Silicon Valley that the current model of AI on your computer is "the worst that you will ever use". This means that the skills required for AI-enabled roles must adapt at pace. This year's training will not be the same as next year's.

Understanding AI legal regimes

Training on relevant AI legal regimes depends on the firm's geographic footprint. Staff in UK-based firms, for example, need to understand the regulator-led UK regime. That said, it is helpful to understand the EU regime, including the AI Act, particularly if clients fall under it. Contracts are also doing the heavy lifting in the UK in the absence of an overarching AI statute.

Understanding any professional conduct obligations

In England and Wales, the Solicitors Regulation Authority's (SRA) *Code of Conduct for Solicitors, RELs, RFLs and RSLs* (SRA Code of Conduct) comprises a "framework for ethical and competent practice".[22] It does not refer specifically to AI, but lawyers are expected to apply its principles when using AI. The SRA states that firms should "introduce, train and operate AI in a way that protects confidentiality" and "train and supervise [their] staff in what is and is not a safe and acceptable use of [their] systems and other uses of AI".[23] Lawyers should keep a keen eye on developments in confidentiality and privilege in particular.

Understanding any relevant standards

The seven principal International Standards Organization (ISO) standards in relation to AI are ISO/IEC 22989, ISO/IEC 42001, ISO/IEC 23894, ISO/IEC 42005, ISO/IEC 42006, ISO/IEC 38507, and ISO/IEC TS 42119-2. Other standards may apply too, such as the National Institute of Standards and Technology's *AI Risk Management Framework*.[24] If these standards apply to AI use in a firm, the relevant aspects should be understood by people in the firm.

Understanding any relevant guidelines or principles

Large suppliers to firms may have their own guidelines or principles, such as Google or Microsoft. Finally, other guidelines may also be relevant, such as the Courts and Tribunals Judiciary's *Artificial Intelligence (AI) – Judicial Guidance (October 2025)*.[25] People need to understand these, where relevant.

Knowing when and when not to use AI

For firms, AI is no longer a differentiator – both external and internal stakeholders increasingly expect its use – but this does not mean it needs to or can be used in all circumstances. Many firms are finding out, through trial and error, what works well and what does not. AI is like a microwave: a remarkable technology that slashes cooking time. It can cook a lot of food, but you still would not use it to bake bread. AI is similarly a tool with many limitations.

Some firms, for example, prohibit putting anything highly confidential into AI, even where data are encrypted and isolated in the client's tenant (ie, "walled off" within a cloud platform), and commitments have been given not to use such data to train any models. Knowledge providers, such as Thomson Reuters and LexisNexis, also limit how their products can be used and what can be input into them. In any training, people should also understand that they must follow any relevant systems where a client has explicitly forbidden AI's use.

Ultimately, AI does not know your clients as well as your lawyers; it cannot formulate judgments enriched by your lawyers' experience. Not having legal personality, it cannot take responsibility for any advice given. There is still a lot that it cannot do, which training needs to reflect.

Junior lawyers need a basic set of AI skills, as set out in this chapter,[26] but more senior lawyers will also need additional skills: knowing how to supervise juniors using AI; understanding what to look for when procuring AI; knowing how to explain a firm's AI use to clients; and so on. Soft skills (discussed below) are also important when working in teams.

Skills for specific roles

We now briefly turn to skills that are relevant to specific roles, such as lawyers and allied professionals. The AI Workforce Consortium is a group of ten global corporations (Accenture, Cisco, Cornerstone, Eightfold, Google, IBM, Indeed, Intel, Microsoft, and SAP) who have developed a skills glossary to help "align job requirements with training programs" and "[empower] individuals to build the right skills".[27] It splits skills into ten categories, from fundamental concepts to "Future Frontiers", which includes quantum machine learning.

Cisco also splits its people into four personas to help create effective AI training: users, enablers, builders, and leaders. Using these or similar taxonomies, firms can determine what skills are necessary for specific roles.

General skills training needs to stress the fact that working in multidisciplinary teams (MDTs) is becoming the norm. MDTs are key to successful AI adoption and, despite what many lawyers think, this includes working with allied professionals.

Lawyers: Understanding hallucinations and misgroundings

Here is a quick test. What is the next number in this sequence: five, ten, 20? Typically, an AI model would answer 40, reasoning that the sequence doubles each time.[28] Statistically, it is the most likely response from the vast datasets LLMs are trained on. The model does not "think" or "know"' the answer like a human does, but it seems to have arrived at the correct one. However, in some contexts, this is incorrect, such as the sequence of UK banknotes: 5 → 10 → 20 → 50.

This is perhaps unfair, as the first example gives no context to help it on its statistical way. However, many LLMs do not help themselves either: rather than seeking clarification, they will happily try to work out the most plausible next character or word. An LLM "knows", for example, what case citations look like, so it can, from time to time, produce fabricated cases that look real, particularly if it has been trained to always give an answer. This is effectively where you get "40" when you were looking for "50".

These "hallucinations" pose a serious risk for lawyers.[29] Researcher Damien Charlotin's AI Hallucination Cases database tracks legal decisions where genAI has produced hallucinated content.[30] It shows a sharp acceleration in hallucination cases from March 2025 onwards. At the time of writing, there were almost 60 cases in the UK alone, and this figure continues to grow.[31]

In *Ayinde v. LB Haringey*,[32] Dame Victoria Sharp P (President of the King's Bench Division) said that those who use AI have a "professional duty" to check for accuracy and that supervisors who do not check the work of a more junior fee-earner are "likely to be more culpable than a lawyer who fails to ensure that his own work is free from such 'hallucinations'".[33]

Hallucinations are not the only game in town; other errors exist too. "Misgrounding" is where a case actually exists and might look "right", but the cited case does not support the claim the lawyer is making.[34] These can be more dangerous than hallucinations, because they are more subtle and tricky to spot.

Lawyers also need to be alert to jurisdictional contamination where, say, US legal concepts are imported via AI models.[35] This is particularly the case with open models not designed for non-US legal markets.

While some firms are experimenting with a "double agent" approach, where one AI model checks the output of another,[36] firms nonetheless need robust systems to ensure that AI is checked for accuracy, including all citations and authorities. As Lewis Silkin notes in its guidance on using AI, the mantra is "validate, validate, validate". Senior lawyers need to be alive to output from juniors which looks "too good to be true"; to challenge it; and to find time to train those junior lawyers who need to develop their professional judgment outside of AI tools.

Aside from the regulatory consequences of lawyers being reported to the SRA, the reputational damage can be costly too.

Lawyers: Knowing how to prompt

Getting the right answer by asking the right question in the right way matters more than ever when dealing with AI. The need to ask well when using AI is also highlighted in the SRA's *Risk Outlook* report on the use of AI,[37] which states that staff should be encouraged "to practice asking effective questions of AI" and firms should "if possible, provide training, to gain the best results".[38]

Enter "prompt engineering", a self-aggrandizing term for the process of inputting instructions in natural language – prompts – into AI models to maximize the chances of getting the desired response. Prompting democratizes AI, bringing its remarkable power to more people than ever. A better term, given that most lawyers are trained in the tradition of the humanities, is perhaps to call prompting the "art of asking" (while there is a science behind prompting, using techniques like zero-shot or chain-of-thought prompting, the art of refining prompts is important too). This might resonate more with certain lawyers.

Depending on the audience, people need to understand:

- What prompting is;
- How to supply basic and more advanced prompts;
- How the same prompt can produce different results;
- How each AI model has its own specific requirements and nuances (some models include functionality that allows users to improve their prompts); and
- That some products no longer require complex prompting techniques.

Libraries of prompts can encourage people to use AI more, but firms need to be aware that prompts can age quickly, particularly when the underlying AI model is updated.

Furthermore, the way in which people interact with AI, via prompting, is changing. The result is that prompting may well become a less important skill in the years to come.

Lawyers: Knowing how to add context and understanding "context drift" and "chunking"

Imagine asking a trainee solicitor to draft a 100-page contract without any context: "Just draft me a sale and purchase agreement." The result is likely to be not much better than the precedent itself. AI needs context, too. This may involve a playbook which helps answer questions such as: what approach does the firm typically take? What approach is acceptable for this transaction or for the market? Sometimes, uploading examples of a desired output can help.

"Context drift" is where an AI model drifts off the point after a certain number of prompts, as if its mind has started to wander. "Chunking" is where users break down large documents into smaller, more manageable pieces for AI models to "digest" better. Although models are improving all the while, firms should consider whether training includes guidance on all the above.

Lawyers: Understanding client behavior

Clients may input data into open AI models when trying to understand their legal rights. They may also use such models to check their lawyer's work. In both cases, they may potentially lose privilege (see, for example, *UK and R (on the application of Munir) v. Secretary of State for the Home Department* [2026][39]). AI-generated evidence and prompt histories may also be admissible. Clients might also use AI to prepare for their meetings with lawyers, sometimes arriving with voluminous amounts of AI-generated material that looks impressive but is not legally sound. Any training program should highlight these challenges and what lawyers should consider doing and advising when such situations may arise.[40]

Allied professionals

This book discusses various allied professionals who work in firms. Some, such as legal engineers and legal data scientists, need a deep and broad knowledge of AI. While AI leaders need the broadest and deepest knowledge of any non-engineering role, other roles need basic AI literacy, in combination with further skills tailored to their specialisms. Many will need specific, practical training on how to leverage AI as part of a firm's service delivery strategy (such as by using tools like SharePoint). Consider uploading the *2025 AI Skills Glossary* from the AI Workforce Consortium[41] to your AI model of choice and relevant job descriptions to create a skills framework for the allied professionals in your firm.

Matters that can be forgotten in skills development

Beyond the role-specific competencies discussed above, several cross-cutting considerations are often overlooked in training programs. These are not tied to any one role but are relevant across firms. These can include the following.

Environmental impact

Many firms place increasing value on environmental, social, and governance (ESG) initiatives (including those in relation to corporate and social responsibility (CSR)) and have developed comprehensive strategies around them. While there is still much uncertainty around the environmental impact of AI,[42] firms need to ensure their AI and ESG strategies align and that their lawyers understand the ESG impact of their AI use and how to minimize it.

Ethical impact

Firms need to be wary of not obsessing about potential AI efficiencies to the detriment of their ethical obligations. In March 2026, the Legal Services Board (LSB) noted that, apart from rules such as the SRA Code of Conduct and guidance, there is "limited bespoke education and training" to help lawyers "specifically identify and understand how to apply their professional ethical duties".[43] The LSB wants a greater focus on ethical practice and has tasked the likes of the SRA to drive this.[44]

Outside of the framework of the SRA, an increasing number of firms have been granted, for example, Certified B Corporation status (B Corp), which means that they have met certain ethics standards on ESG. Such firms' AI strategies need to be in line with the standards they are obligated to uphold.

Finally, while firms consider the ethical challenges of using AI, they will increasingly consider the ethical risk of *not* using it. Is using AI in the client's best interests? If so, would it be unethical not to use it? These questions will increasingly arise.

Cybersecurity risks

AI can enable faster detection of cyberthreats and help defenses adapt, but it can turbocharge cyberattacks too. In the rush to use AI, cybersecurity must never be overlooked. Training is key to raising awareness of AI security threats, including on emerging risks, such as prompt injection.

The UK's Department for Science, Innovation and Technology's *Guidance: Code of Practice for the Cyber Security of AI* states that training should be "regularly reviewed and updated"[45] and "tailored to the specific roles and responsibilities of staff members".[46] Other guidance stresses the need for training, such as the Guidelines for secure AI system development by the UK National Cyber Security Centre and the US Cybersecurity and Infrastructure Security Agency.

Soft skills

Lewis Silkin, in its *Future @ Work* report, noted that it is not just technical skills that firms need to embed: "Uniquely human attributes, such as judgment, creativity, collaboration, communication, and system thinking, are viewed as the skills that will ultimately enable technology to deliver lasting value, with organizations anticipating a much greater need for soft skills (64 percent) over technical skills (15 percent)."[47] Firms need to help individuals and teams (particularly junior lawyers) develop their "muscle memory" for these skills.

The cultural and behavioral factors that drive successful AI adoption

The chapter now turns to an equally important question: how firms create the conditions in which the above skills are put to use. Technical competence alone is not enough – without the right culture and behaviors, even well-trained teams will struggle to adopt AI effectively.

The maturity of AI adoption varies across firms. Often this is deliberate: some have taken a firm-wide approach, whereas others have focused on use cases in certain teams. Whatever the approach, AI adoption should not be taken for granted. The *Future @ Work* report noted that almost half of organizations (49 percent) "expect cultural resistance to slow down the adoption of new technologies and the implementation of new operating models".[48]

Below are some of the key factors which are likely to drive successful adoption, some of which are often overlooked. Early momentum on these factors is likely to pay dividends later.

Be strategic and tactical

You might have an AI strategy or a data strategy, or both. This is the "why" and "what" that you want to achieve. However, you need an overarching firm strategy to put them into context.

Strategy allows clarity of purpose: what is the firm looking to achieve with AI? Answering this makes it much easier to understand how to drive successful adoption. The AI strategy and data strategy, as applicable, should also tie in with any other relevant strategies which the firm has or is developing, such as those of its business teams, legal practice groups, sector groups, and so on.

Firms need to be tactical, too, and plan out how to achieve the strategies:

- Take AI procurement. Suppliers sell urgency: "Buy now before your competitors do!" However, you need to be tactical on timing. If you buy an AI product before it can be properly integrated into your systems, expecting it to be adopted is naive at best. At worst, it is likely to be costly, and your people may fall back to using unauthorized AI ("shadow AI").
- An unstructured "big bang" roll-out of AI can be a poor tactic too, overloading teams and making it difficult to learn from early adopters. Running targeted pilots enables firms to see what works and what does not.

Take a top-down approach

Napoleon Bonaparte is reported to have said that leaders are "dealers in hope".[49] As with any large-scale change, they need to tell a good story; articulate a positive vision of AI use; and deal with the fear that AI engenders in many lawyers (see the discussion on fighting the fear below). They need to use AI themselves, be seen doing so, and champion its use. A strong and consistent comms plan is vital. To drive AI use, firms should look to make AI a standing item in leadership meetings, away days, partner conferences, and the like.

Furthermore, the structure of many firms means that one partner or a cohort of partners can stymie progress. It is vital to understand the personalities in your firm. As the author noted in *Legal Practice in the Digital Age*, "forcing technology and innovation onto unwilling colleagues, without understanding the archetypal dynamics, is a risky strategy. Each archetype has a role to play, even the sceptics from time to time."[50]

Firms, and their leaders, need to ensure they take their responsibilities to have proper systems in place under professional conduct rules seriously. Proper governance gives lawyers increased confidence in using AI tools. This was highlighted in *Ayinde v. LB Haringey*.[51] In light of the above, as the *Future @ Work* report notes, 44 percent of organizations are "strengthening leadership capability & governance structures to address capability gaps".[52]

Take a bottom-up approach, too

"At the coalface": the metaphorical place where abstract theory hits messy reality. As much thought needs to go to supporting and training the teams doing day-to-day work with AI on the ground. Examples of best practice to consider include:

- *Appointing "super-users" (or "power-users"):* These are users who are especially curious about AI and experiment extensively with it. They have no formal qualifications in AI, but they see opportunities to integrate AI into their daily workflows and proactively look for new ones. Research indicates, paradoxically, that such super-users end up doing more hours, but they reportedly do so voluntarily, as they find their work more engaging (however, beware of "brain fry" – see our discussion of cognitive overload below).[53]
- *Appointing AI champions who engage their teams in using AI:* Champions build up a buzz about the technology and how it can be used. They showcase easy wins to colleagues and are the go-to people for any day-to-day queries. They help others get past the barrier of "If no one else is using it, why should I?"
- *Setting up sharing sessions:* Such sessions highlight use cases, prompts, and workflows. They are also a great opportunity to showcase examples of better outcomes, more client work, or reduced write-offs. The author's firm recently, for example, undertook ideation sessions at an away day on what AI might be able do.
- *Setting up "walled gardens" in which to experiment safely:* Seeing is believing. People are often afraid of learning about AI on live systems for fear of "breaking them".

Beware of AI hype

For some AI tools, marketing has reached stratospheric levels of hyperbole. Products are spoken about in reverential tones, as though we have just landed on Mars for the first time. Additionally, there are the inevitable LinkedIn posts offering yet another specific take on AI and why you need to do something about it *now* with *this* product before it is *too late*! This sugar rush of AI hype is not helping the profession. Firms risk crashing and burning when adopting new AI tools. Expectations are often too high. Firms, therefore, need to take a measured approach: training should be honest about what specific AI tools can and cannot do (research in a healthcare context also indicates that a healthy skepticism of AI means that users are more vigilant[54]). Lawyers are trained to be skeptical, so honesty fosters trust and thus adoption. Without trust in the AI tools or the senior leadership teams implementing them, the tools risk gathering virtual dust on virtual shelves as expensive "shelfware".

Nudge your people

Behavioral science is a rich source of insight to help drive adoption. The Behavioural Insights Team (BIT) – a UK-based global research and innovation consultancy once known as the "Nudge Unit" – focuses on understanding human behavior to facilitate and embed change. It publishes frameworks such as EAST, which firms can use to make adoption easy, attractive, simple, and timely. On AI, BIT reiterates: "The real challenge, and the greatest opportunity, is a human one."

Firms should also concentrate, as all good marketers do, on the benefits of using AI, rather than its features. "Cut the time you take to do X" resonates more than "Our AI has the following specifications..."

Nurture human intelligence

In the rush to adopt AI, human intelligence must be prioritized too. AI is about people *and* AI, not people *or* AI. However, the evidence indicates that our human intelligence is suffering. In 2025, LawCare, the mental health charity for the legal profession, found that 59.1 percent of those surveyed had "poor mental wellbeing".[55] Dr Hannah Critchlow in the *21st Century Brain* reminds us that, in our brains of "86 trillion connections,"[56] we already have "all the cognitive skills we need to flourish in the decades to come".[57] AI will, in theory, free up time for more strategic thinking. However, humans are not robots. It is often in our downtime, when our minds wander, that we come up with our best ideas.

The upshot? We need to support our people to look after their brains and mental health by keeping physically active and eating and resting well. We also need to keep an eye on how AI-powered workflows impact on our people and, if needs be, to consider new approaches to rest and recovery. Ultimately, we need to learn how to live intelligently alongside AI. Successful AI adoption requires us to be holistic in our approach.

Tell stories

Humans are hardwired for stories – we love the who, what, when, where, why, and how. The good news? Stories are fundamentally about change – think about how popular TED Talks are, and their strapline: "Ideas change everything." When telling the story of AI (and the matters referred to in this chapter), it helps to stir emotions so that they resonate, but avoid using hackneyed images of AI robots.

Fight the fear

When it comes to AI, people can smell change in the air, like the earthy scent that heralds a summer thunderstorm. However, storms, while scary, can be exciting, too. They clear the air and help seeds to germinate. At the moment, it feels like we are still awaiting the storm. "Prepare for an AI jobs apocalypse," one article in *The Economist* warns.[58] Others predict the end of civilization as we know it.

Fear helps to protect us from danger, but it also affects our ability to think long-term. Training about AI needs to be honest and free from hyperbole. It should clarify what AI can and cannot do: it is an augmentative tool for lawyers, not a replacement for their expertise. It also needs to clarify that it is perfectly reasonable to be both pessimistic and optimistic, worried and excited about AI at the same time, depending on which aspect you're considering. Breathless naivety or world-weary skepticism are both unhelpful.

Fear can manifest itself at a micro – as opposed to macro – level too. Lawyers are likely to be concerned about billing targets if the time that it takes to do a task is materially shortened and the amount that can be charged is thereby lessened. The result? They shy away from using this technology.

Finally, one certain way of scaring your people is using, in the words of Better Images of AI – a project that provides free, alternative images representing AI and its societal impacts – hackneyed images of "humanoid robots, glowing brains, outstretched robot hands, blue backgrounds, and the Terminator".[59] This initiative, backed by the likes of the BBC, encourages organizations to use less stereotyped images of AI which, for example, do not "sow fear".[60]

Challenges of embedding new tools into real workflows

Firms must also confront the practical challenges of embedding AI into the day-to-day practice of law This section examines the challenges.

In the practice of law, tasks for which AI is commonly used in firms include:

- Drafting;
- Document automation;
- Document review and analysis;
- Document summarization; and
- Legal research.

Embedding AI into these tasks raises many practical challenges, particularly integration with other platforms. The discussion below address several challenges that deserve closer attention.

Recognize that it is about tasks, and not jobs

The author spoke to Roch Glowacki, partner at Lewis Silkin. He suggests thinking about our roles as consisting of "tasks A to Z". AI might "be really good at doing tasks B, F, Y and W". This means, for task A, you work normally. You then "dip into AI" for B before resuming your normal workflow at C, and so on.

A useful resource on job redesign (including training needs) is *The Guide to Job Redesign in the Age of AI*, published by the Infocomm Media Development Authority and Personal Data Protection Commission in Singapore.[61] It includes a methodology of:

- Breaking down roles into tasks;
- Considering AI's potential impact on each task;
- Considering whether AI should be implemented for each task; and
- Working with managers and employees to determine what tasks are valuable to them.

Be wary of productivity claims

Economist Robert Solow once quipped: "You can see the computer age everywhere but in the productivity statistics."[62] This is the "Solow paradox": advances in technology don't always translate into productivity gains – at least, not initially. Research in 2025 suggests that this paradox applies to AI too – for now.[63]

The author suggests that AI could well result in more work in firms: a greater ability to process documents means more drafting, more markup, more Teams calls (with AI-generated meeting notes and action lists), and more emails, as our current technology no longer acts as a brake on what we can do. In April 2026, Lord Briggs said that AI is "likely to lead to a tsunami of small to moderate value civil claims, once litigants are enabled by OpenAI to formulate them without lawyers".[64] However, using our judgment, giving advice and negotiating is something that AI largely cannot accelerate. When embedding workflows, firms need to be aware of not squeezing out these tasks, as it is typically these (non-AI) tasks that are of most value to clients.

Furthermore, initial research indicates that, while AI can feel like it is supercharging productivity, it may sometimes have the opposite effect. In early 2025, research nonprofit METR undertook a survey in which developers believed AI made them 20 percent faster; however, task completion times were found to be almost 20 percent longer.[65] AI also enables us to do new things we could not do before. In May 2026, further research published on Model Evaluation & Threat Research noted that people would do well to focus more on the value that AI can bring – such as more complex analysis – as opposed to just the speed of delivery.[66] Further peer-reviewed research is needed in this important area, particularly given that many studies on productivity involve self-reported data from users or are sponsored or written by AI vendors.

Firms need to be conscious of productivity claims when redesigning workflows and pricing models, particularly given that clients relying on overstated productivity gains may apply fee pressure on their firms.

Recognize that AI implementation is a never-ending, not one-off project

AI is not a one-off transformation program; rather, it is a never-ending project comprising tasks such as fixing siloed data and poor-quality data. Firms' planning cycles are more iterative than ever. A report published by The Positive Group, *The AI Leadership Challenge in Law*, notes: "AI is often introduced into existing workflows without fundamentally redesigning how work is organized."[67] The pressures of time-recording can mean lawyers are unable to find the time needed to rethink workflows. The result? Existing ways of working are reinforced, which can result in new tools being piled onto them.

Be aware of "cognitive overload"

Firms should be aware of what some academics call "brain fry"[68]: "cognitive overload", in which people use AI excessively. There is a sweet spot in the efficiency of AI use, which can be impacted if there is too much switching between tasks. Successful AI adoption recognizes that productivity is typically nuanced.

Use AI tools to create workflows

Many AI tools come with workflows that can be developed further. Some AI suppliers, such as Harvey, recognize that firms could do more in this area. In a report published in November 2025, *Defining the Impact of Legal AI: How Harvey Customers Realise Value*,[69] Harvey notes that "workflow builder is seen as having potential, but fewer use cases were reported". Now known as "agent builder," this is a tool which allows subscribers to publish reusable, shareable workflows for teams to run. Firms should determine whether they can leverage this functionality to their advantage.

Use your imagination

There has never been a better time to rethink workflows. Lawyers don't have to sit in front of screens typing all day. Roch Glowacki described an example in which he used voice functionality in his AI tool to review a complex contract rather than typing. He printed the contract out, placed it in front of him, opened Harvey, and asked it to "keep a running tab" of all his thoughts that he was going to dictate while reviewing this contract. He asked the AI tool to split it into three buckets: (1) points or questions for the client; (2) things he needed to research or double-check; and (3) changes he wanted to make to the contract. After resolving the items in Bucket 2, he turned Bucket 1 into a draft email and only then moved onto Bucket 3, which Harvey then implemented as a high-level redline for him to consider. Throughout the process, he worked through each bucket, reorganizing items and asking Harvey to cross-check points within the contract and research on the internet where necessary. Roch reflected that, while the time saving may not have been "revolutionary", the approach yielded greater confidence in the output because "it was a hybrid approach of me and AI" and it increased his job satisfaction because "there was less friction. [He] enjoyed it more".

How firms approach training and capability development

The previous sections have examined what skills are needed; what cultural conditions support adoption; and what practical challenges arise when AI is embedded into workflows. The final section turns to the question of delivery: how should firms approach the training and capability development that underpins all the above?

AI literacy, and the training and capability development underpinning it, is like painting the Forth Bridge: less about achieving an idealized finished state, and more about recognizing that it requires ongoing maintenance – and continuous investment, both in terms of time and money.[70] A clear AI strategy, backed by a robust governance framework, helps to ensure that training and capability development form part of sustained organizational change, rather than being treated as a one-off tech rollout. This also helps minimize the risks of unauthorized – or "shadow" – AI use.

At the time of writing, many firms remain at a relatively early stage of their training journey. Drawing upon discussions with fellow members of the TEDLaw International Advisory Board, the author's experience suggests that formal AI training remains the exception, rather than the rule. In most firms, training tends to be self-directed, ad-hoc and informal, supplemented, in some instances, by supplier-led training. Larger firms tend to have more formalized programs. Lewis Silkin, for example, has created an AI literacy eLearning product in collaboration with AI governance platform, Holistic AI. This is offered at two levels, depending on a team's technical knowledge and context of AI use, and helps ensure compliance with the AI literacy requirements of the EU AI Act.

Training is not just about setting out the risks and opportunities of AI; it should also be practical in nature and offer real-world insights and examples. FutureDotNow (in partnership with BIT and with the support of the Department for Science, Innovation and Technology) published a paper in June 2025, *Learning that clicks*,[71] setting out nine recommended actions, six promising actions, and four discouraged actions for organizations looking to improve digital capability. From the author's experience, the following can be particularly effective for firms:

- *Create role-specific content, where possible:* What works for trainee solicitors may be different to what works for the senior leadership team.
- *Use "bite-size" formats:* Short, focused sessions (such as pre-recorded videos on an intranet) can often be more effective than hour-long sessions. Think about how effective a 10-minute, one-to-one chat with an AI champion can be.
- *Create dedicated time for some or all of the training:* Lawyers need protected time, free from billing targets, so that they can truly focus their minds.

Finally, look at what other firms are doing. Speak with your contacts to see what works and what does not. Some firms are collaborating on best practice in AI training, such as the Global Legal Tech Alliance. That said, most firms in the UK develop their own AI training, often with help from technology providers.

Conclusion

AI is eroding the scarcity value of many aspects of human intelligence. Intelligence is increasingly no longer our privilege alone. What's more, AI does not need a coffee or lunch break. It never gets tired and never complains. Our whole society, and the legal profession, is built on the premise that humans have the monopoly on intelligence. This assumption is now obsolete: intelligence is becoming a commodity. Of course, like all profound disruptions, this can be scary, messy, and, at times, discombobulating. However, it also promises to unlock opportunities at a scale that we have scarcely begun to appreciate.

References

1 Internet Archive, "Microsoft Windows 95 Video Guide (1995) [Full VHS Tape]", 3 December 2018. See: https://archive.org/details/MicrosoftWindows95VideoGuide.

2 *Ibid.*

3 Arbuckle A, "The launch of Windows 95", Mashable, 24 August 2015. See: https://mashable.com/archive/windows-95-launch.

4 Wired, "May 26, 1995: Gates, Microsoft Jump on 'Internet Tidal Wave'", 26 May 2018. See: https://www.wired.com/2010/05/0526bill-gates-internet-memo/.

5 Milmo D, "ChatGPT reaches 100 million users two months after launch", *The Guardian*, 2 February 2023. See: https://www.theguardian.com/technology/2023/feb/02/chatgpt-100-million-users-open-ai-fastest-growing-app.

6 Nadella S, "Looking ahead: 2026", SN Scratchpad, 29 December 2025. See: https://snscratchpad.com/posts/looking-ahead-2026/.

7 Vos G, "Speech by the Master of the Rolls: AI – Transforming the work of lawyers and judges", Courts and Tribunals Judiciary, 11 March 2024. See: https://www.judiciary.uk/speech-by-the-master-of-the-rolls-ai-transforming-the-work-of-lawyers-and-judges/.

8 KPMG CEO Outlook, "KPMG 2025 CEO Outlook – UK", KPMG, 2025. See: https://kpmg.com/uk/en/insights/strategy/kpmg-ceo-outlook-uk.html.

9 Lewis Silkin, *Future @ Work 2026: Building for future readiness*, February 2026. See: https://www.lewissilkin.com/our-thinking/future-of-work-hub/insights/2026/02/04/future-at-work-2026-report.

10 AI Workforce Consortium, *ICT in Motion: The Next Wave of AI Integration* (2025), Cisco, 2025. See: https://www.cisco.com/content/dam/cisco-cdc/site/m/ai-workforce-consortium/documents/2025-ai-workforce-consortium-full-report.pdf.

11 Berger W, "Why Curious People Are Destined for the C-Suite", *Harvard Business Review*, 11 September 2015. See: https://hbr.org/2015/09/why-curious-people-are-destined-for-the-c-suite.

12 Aksenov P, "Stanislav Petrov: The man who may have saved the world", BBC News, 26 September 2013. See: https://www.bbc.com/news/world-europe-24280831

13 *Ibid.*

14 LexisNexis, *The mentorship gap*, 2 February 2026. See: https://www.lexisnexis.co.uk/research-and-reports/the-mentorship-gap.html.

15 University of Bath, "University of Bath study warns AI could erode human capital, thinking and expertise in the workplace", 1 April 2026. See: https://www.bath.ac.uk/announcements/university-of-bath-study-warns-ai-could-erode-human-capital-thinking-and-expertise-in-the-workplace.

16 Hardman P, "The Cognitive Offloading Paradox", Substack, 16 April 2026. See: https://drphilippahardman.substack.com/p/the-cognitive-offloading-paradox?.

17 UK Jurisdictional Taskforce, "Public consultation – Liability for AI Harms under the private law of England and Wales", Lawtech UK, 2026. See: https://lawtechuk.io/ukjt/public-consultation-liability-for-ai-harms-under-the-private-law-of-england-and-wales/.

18 MIT AI Risk Initiative, "AI Risk Navigator", Massachusetts Institute of Technology, 2026. See: https://www.airi-navigator.com/.

19 Sajadieh S, Fattorini L, Perrault R et al, *Artificial Intelligence Index Annual Report 2026*, Stanford University Institute for Human-Centered Artificial Intelligence, April 2026. See: https://hai.stanford.edu/ai-index/2026-ai-index-report%C2%A0.

20 An AI consultant at the University of Oxford's AI Competency Centre, Kelly Webb-Davies, has developed a framework of five AI personas that help users interact with LLMs in "a memorable way" to "think critically about their AI use". See: https://kellywebbdavies.com/aipersonas/.

21 Sajadieh S, Fattorini L, Perrault R et al, *Artificial Intelligence Index Annual Report* 2026, Stanford University Institute for Human-Centered Artificial Intelligence, April 2026. See: https://hai.stanford.edu/ai-index/2026-ai-index-report%C2%A0.

22 Solicitors Regulation Authority, "SRA Code of Conduct for Solicitors, RELs, RFLs and RSLs", 16 December 2024. See: https://www.sra.org.uk/solicitors/standards-regulations/code-conduct-solicitors/.

23 Solicitors Regulation Authority, "Risk Outlook report: The use of artificial intelligence in the legal market", 20 November 2023. See: https://www.sra.org.uk/sra/research-publications/artificial-intelligence-legal-market/.

24 National Institute of Standards and Technology, *AI Risk Management Framework*, United States Department of Commerce, January 2023. See: https://www.nist.gov/itl/ai-risk-management-framework.

25 Courts and Tribunals Judiciary, *Artificial Intelligence (AI) – Judicial Guidance (October 2025)*, 31 October 2025. See: https://www.judiciary.uk/guidance-and-resources/artificial-intelligence-ai-judicial-guidance-october-2025/.

26 The Lady Chief Justice, the Baroness Carr of Walton-on-the-Hill, in a speech at Mansion House in London on 2 July 2025, referred to the need for "more training and support for lawyers, particularly trainees and those in the early years of their careers, to enable them to use AI circumspectly and usefully". See: Lascelles Carr S, "Mansion House speech by the Lady Chief Justice", Courts and Tribunals Judiciary, 3 July 2025. See: https://www.judiciary.uk/mansion-house-speech-by-the-lady-chief-justice-2/.

27 AI Workforce Consortium, "Preparing for the Future: AI's Impact on Information and Communication Technology Jobs", Cisco,2026. See: https://www.cisco.com/site/m/ai-workforce-consortium/index.html.

28 Tested using Harvey on 18 May 2026.

29 Magesh V, Surani D, Dahl M et al, "Hallucination-Free? Assessing the Reliability of Leading AI Legal Research Tools", *Journal of Empirical Legal Studies*, 2025, volume 22, issue 2, pp. 216–242. https://doi.org/10.1111/jels.12413.

30 Charlotin D, "AI Hallucination Cases", 2026. See: https://www.damiencharlotin.com/hallucinations/.

31 As of 27 May 2026.

32 *Ayinde v. LB Haringey* [2025] EWHC 1383 (Admin).

33 *R (on the application of Munir) v. Secretary of State for the Home Department)* [2026] UKUT 00081 (IAC).

34 Magesh V, Surani D, Dahl M et al, "Hallucination-Free? Assessing the Reliability of Leading AI Legal Research Tools", *Journal of Empirical Legal Studies*, 2025, volume 22, issue 2, pp. 216–242. https://doi.org/10.1111/jels.12413. https://onlinelibrary.wiley.com/doi/full/10.1111/jels.12413?msockid=1d84be73c55567c70822a8abc482665b. Additionally, see: Ullah K, "The AI Legal Problem Nobody Is Talking About — And It Is More Dangerous Than Hallucinations", LinkedIn, 6 May 2026. See: https://www.linkedin.com/pulse/ai-legal-problem-nobody-talking-more-dangerous-than-kalim-ullah-101if.

35 Magesh V, Surani D, Dahl M et al, "Hallucination-Free? Assessing the Reliability of Leading AI Legal Research Tools", *Journal of Empirical Legal Studies*, 2025, volume 22, issue 2, pp. 216–242. https://doi.org/10.1111/jels.12413.

36 Doyle C, "SullCrom can't blame AI – here's what firms do now", *The Lawyer*, 30 April 2026. See: https://www.thelawyer.com/sullcrom-cant-blame-ai-heres-what-firms-do-now/.

37 Solicitors Regulation Authority, "Risk Outlook report: The use of artificial intelligence in the legal market", 20 November 2023. See: https://www.sra.org.uk/sra/research-publications/artificial-intelligence-legal-market/.

38 *Ibid.*

39 Lindsley F, "[2026] UKUT 00081", Tribunal Decisions, 19 February 2026. See: https://tribunalsdecisions.service.gov.uk/utiac/2026-ukut-00081..

40 The Bar Standards Board's *Guidance on the use of Artificial Intelligence and Other Technologies*, published in May 2026, reiterates this requirement.
41 AI Workforce Constortium, *2025 AI Skills Glossary*, Cisco, 2025. See: https://www.cisco.com/content/dam/cisco-cdc/site/m/ai-workforce-consortium/documents/2025-AI-skills-glossary.pdf.
42 See, for example: Gayle D, "Officials hugely underestimated impact of AI datacentres on UK carbon emissions", *The Guardian*, 24 April 2026. See: https://www.theguardian.com/technology/2026/apr/24/officials-hugely-underestimated-impact-of-ai-datacentres-on-uk-carbon-emissions. Additionally, see: Hunt E, "We asked experts about the most responsible ways to use AI tools – here's what they said", *The Guardian*, 18 March 2026. See: https://www.theguardian.com/lifeandstyle/ng-interactive/2026/mar/18/how-to-use-ai-tools-expert-guide.
43 Legal Services Board, *Statement of policy on upholding professional ethical duties*, 22 May 2026. See: https://legalservicesboard.org.uk/wp-content/uploads/2026/03/LSB-Upholding-Professional-Ethical-Duties-March-2026.pdf.
44 Solicitors Regulation Authority, "SRA corporate strategy 2023–2026", 1 November 2023. See: https://www.sra.org.uk/sra/corporate-strategy/.
45 Department for Science, Innovation and Technology, *Guidance: Code of Practice for the Cyber Security of AI*, 31 January 2025. See: https://www.gov.uk/government/publications/ai-cyber-security-code-of-practice/code-of-practice-for-the-cyber-security-of-ai; Birrs C, " Speech by the Chancellor of the High Court: Legal professional privilege in the Age of AI", Courts and Tribunals Judiciary, 24 April 2026. See: https://www.judiciary.uk/speech-by-the-chancellor-of-the-high-court-legal-professional-privilege-in-the-age-of-ai/; and Department for Science, Innovation and Technology, "Cyber Resilience Pledge declaration", 22 April 2026. See: https://www.gov.uk/government/publications/cyber-resilience-pledge/cyber-resilience-pledge-declaration.
46 Department for Science, Innovation and Technology, *Guidance: Code of Practice for the Cyber Security of AI*, 31 January 2025. See: https://www.gov.uk/government/publications/ai-cyber-security-code-of-practice/code-of-practice-for-the-cyber-security-of-ai.
47 Lewis Silkin, *Future @ Work 2026: Building for future readiness*, February 2026. See: https://www.lewissilkin.com/our-thinking/future-of-work-hub/insights/2026/02/04/future-at-work-2026-report.
48 *Ibid.*
49 Attributed to Napoleon Bonaparte; primary source untraced.
50 Caddy P, Jackson D and Randle T, *Legal Practice in the Digital Age*, Globe Law and Business; 2023: p. 369.
51 *Ayinde v. LB Haringey* [2025] EWHC 1383 (Admin).

52 Lewis Silkin, *Future @ Work 2026: Building for future readiness*, February 2026. See: https://www.lewissilkin.com/our-thinking/future-of-work-hub/insights/2026/02/04/future-at-work-2026-report.

53 Ranganathan A and Ye XM, "AI Doesn't Reduce Work – It Intensifies It", *Harvard Business Review*, 9 February 2026. See: https://hbr.org/2026/02/ai-doesnt-reduce-work-it-intensifies-it.

54 Fussell DA, Tang CC, Sternhagen J et al, "AI Efficacy as a Function of Trainee Interpreter Proficiency: Lessons from a Randomized Controlled Trial", *American Journal of Neuroradiology*, 2024. https://doi.org/10.3174/ajnr.A8387.

55 LawCare, *Life in the Law Report 2025*, 2025. See: https://lawcare.org.uk/wp-content/uploads/2025/09/Life-in-the-Law-2025.pdf.

56 Critchlow H, *The 21st Century Brain*, London: Transworld Publishers: 2026: p. 5.

57 *Ibid*, p. 4.

58 *The Economist*, "Prepare for an AI jobs apocalypse", 14 May 2026. See: https://www.economist.com/leaders/2026/05/14/prepare-for-an-ai-jobs-apocalypse. However, the *Future @ Work* report says that those surveyed are "more expecting net job creation rather than loss".

59 Better Images of AI, "Have you noticed that news stories and marketing material about Artificial Intelligence are typically illustrated with clichéd and misleading images?", 2026. See: https://betterimagesofai.org/.

60 *Ibid.*

61 Infocomm Media Development Authority and Personal Data Protection Commission, *A Guide to Job Redesign in the Age of AI*, 2020. See: https://file.go.gov.sg/ai-guide-to-jobredesign.pdf.

62 Solow R, "We'd better watch out", *New York Times Book Review*, 12 July 1987.

63 Azhar S, Zhang Z and Lu S, "Empirical Analysis of the Solow Paradox in Artificial Intelligence", *Open Journal of Business and Management*, 2025, volume 13, pp. 3716–3729. https://doi.org/10.4236/ojbm.2025.135200. Additionally, see: Northcote Parkinson C, "Parkinson's Law", *The Economist*, 19 November 1955. See: www.economist.com/news/1955/11/19/parkinsons-law.

64 Briggs M, " Perfect Law Conference On Global Class Actions and Mass Torts", Supreme Court of the United Kingdom, 21 April 2026. See: https://supremecourt.uk/speeches/speech-lord-briggs-21042026.

65 Becker J, Rush N, Barnes B and Rein D, "Measuring the Impact of Early-2025 AI on Experienced Open-Source Developer Productivity", Model Evaluation & Threat Research, 10 July 2025. See: https://metr.org/Early_2025_AI_Experienced_OS_Devs_Study-paper.pdf.

66 METR, "AI Usage Survey" (METR, 11 May 2026), https://metr.org/blog/2026-05-11-ai-usage-survey/. See also: https://www.ft.com/content/197acda2-028f-484e-9489-140443289bbf

67 Positive Group, *The AI Leadership Challenge in Law: The Leadership Behaviours Shaping the Future of Legal Practice*, 2026. See: https://repository.positivegroup.org/media/The-AI-Leadership-Challenge-in-Law.pdf.

68 Bedard J, Kropp M, Hsu M et al, "When Using AI Leads to "Brain Fry"", *Harvard Business Review*, 5 March 2026. See: https://hbr.org/2026/03/when-using-ai-leads-to-brain-fry.

69 Harvey and RSGI, *Defining the Impact of Legal AI: How Harvey Customers Realise Value*, Harvey AI, November 2025. See: https://www.harvey.ai/resources/reports/harvey-rsgi-report#form.

70 The author recognizes that the analogy is a bit weaker, given that painting of the bridge is currently in abeyance: BBC News, "Forth Bridge painting 'is coming to an end'", 5 September 2011. See: https://www.bbc.co.uk/news/uk-scotland-edinburgh-east-fife-14789036.

71 FutureDotNow, Behavioural Insights Team and the Department for Science, Innovation and Technology, *Learning that clicks*, FutureDotNow, June 2025. See: https://futuredotnow.uk/learning-that-clicks/.

About Globe Law and Business

Globe Law and Business was established in 2005. From the very beginning, we set out to create legal books that are sufficiently high level to be of real use to the experienced professional, yet still accessible and easy to navigate. Most of our authors are drawn from Magic Circle and other top commercial firms, both in the United Kingdom and internationally. Our titles are carefully produced, with the utmost attention paid to editorial, design and production processes. We hope this results in high-quality publications that are easy to read and a pleasure to own.

In 2021, we were very pleased to announce the start of a new chapter for Globe Law and Business following the acquisition of law books under the imprint Ark Publishing. Our law firm management list is now significantly expanded with many well-known and loved Ark Publishing titles.

We are also pleased to announce the launch of our online content platform, Globe Law Online, which allows for easy access across firms. Details of all titles included can be found at www.globelawonline.com. Email glo@globelawandbusiness.com for further details and to arrange a free trial for you or your firm.

We'd very much like to hear from you with your thoughts and ideas for improving what we offer. Please do feel free to email me on sian@globelawandbusiness.com. Happy reading and thank you for your time.

Sian O'Neill
Managing director
Globe Law and Business
www.globelawandbusiness.com

www.ingramcontent.com/pod-product-compliance
Lightning Source LLC
LaVergne TN
LVHW051219180726
843446LV00008B/65